THE
Picky
Eater

60 YEARS IN CANADA

19 33
19 93

HarperCollins

THE
Picky
Eater

RECIPES AND SURVIVAL TIPS FOR PARENTS OF FUSSY EATERS

SHARON E. McKAY

A Today's Parent Book
HarperPerennial
HarperCollins*Publishers*Ltd

A working mom is as good as her child care. My sincere thanks to Dana Harrison and her support staff—Cody and Deanna and Bill for taking such good care of The Toad during the writing of this book.

And to Matthew Redman, my inspiration.

Interior illustrations © 1993 by Marilyn Mets.

First Edition

Canadian Cataloguing in Publication Data

McKay, Sharon E.
    The picky eater : recipes and survival tips for parents of fussy eaters

"A Today's Parent book".
ISBN 0-00-637898-6

1. Cookery.   2. Children – Nutrition.   I. Title.

TX652.M44 1993   641.5'622   C92-095784-6

---

93 94 95 96 97 ❖ CW 10 9 8 7 6 5 4 3 2 1

CONTENTS

ACKNOWLEDGMENTS

I would like to thank:

Phillipa (Pippa) Campsie for the idea, the support and the laughter;

Evelyn Raab, senior food writer for *Today's Parent* magazine for reviewing the recipes in this book;

the children and their families who tested the recipes: Julie Creighton, friend, toy consultant and foodie; Jennifer Webber, Matthew and Haley; Karen Gillespie, Meghan, Emily and Jack; Heidi McKay, Nichole and Dave; Trina Tulk, Jeffery, Corrina and Jim; Patty Lowshaw, Casey, Corey and Jim; Janice Gittings, Erica, Andrew and Phil; Lisa Valerioto, Danielle, Nicole, Michael and Tony; Cindy Gekiere, Caitlin and Amanda; Zel Hopson, Jody, Jackie and Loyd; Faye Jordan, Adia, Evan and Eric; Henny McNobb, Alyssa and Keith; Manuella Marchmont, Stephanie, Jeffrey and Mike; Heather Morton, Cameron, Christopher and David; Cathy MacDonald, James and Kristen; Erika Rodman, Christopher, Matthew, Clair and Peter; Dympna Dewar, Sarah, Kathy, Neil and Neil;

Mary Etta McGraw, Fran Hobbs and Mary Pollock for their combined efforts in producing Puppy Chew!;

Dorothy McKay, my mom, who tested just about everything;

and a special thanks to the grade 2 class of Rolph Road School: Kirby, Stephanie, Jenny, Maggie, Paige, Sean, Lauralee, Cole, Colt, James, Michelle, Daniel, Colin, Jeffrey, Matthew, Tiffany, Diana, Lindsay, Cameron and their teacher Mrs. Meg Best;

and to Sam and Joe and David and Sterling;

On the professional side my thanks go to:

Bev Topping, Publisher of *Today's Parent* magazine; Pam Collacott, author *Pam's Kitchen* (Macmillan); Denise Beatty R.P.Dt., nutritionist who read the manuscript with nutrition in mind; Susan Daglish, The Allergy Foundation of Toronto; Karen Balko, Dietitian, Child Health Unit, Doctor's Hospital, Toronto, Ontario;

Those who read the manuscript and lent their comments:

Rena Mendleson, D.Sc., Professor of Nutrition; Dr. William James, Pediatrician, Ottawa; Dr. Miriam Kaufman, Department of Pediatrics, The Hospital for Sick Children, Toronto, Ontario;

and, of course, the editorial team at HarperCollins—Barbara Berson, Laura Krakowec and Editor-in-Chief, Iris Skeoch; and my copy editor, Rosemary Campsie.

INTRODUCTION

I was so smug—the parent one loves to hate. My firstborn was, and is, the perfect eater. Yep, he'll taste and eat almost anything, anywhere, anytime. We can, and do, take him to all sorts of restaurants. "A little gravy with your reindeer meat, young sir?" Of course. "And how about those minced kidneys?" Delicious. "Extra (raw) octopus?" Oh please.

He asked for, and got, a delectable jar of escargots in his Christmas stocking one year. What a child.

I was so proud.

I took full credit.

Time has a way of dealing with the smug. Along came Baby Number 2. This child doesn't eat a thing. Nothing. Zip. I don't care what his doctor says, or how big and healthy he is, he lives on air. I swear. Honest. If his plate is clean, the dog is full.

What's worse, I can't even rest on my laurels. Son Number 1 turned nine and decided that, while he is indeed a "trying kid" (his phrase, but I like it), he now wants to eat only "real food" (food that requires fork, spoon and possibly knife) at dinner. And no breakfast, thanks. He's just not, you know, in the mood for breakfast at 7:30. I'm calm. I explain the need we all have for breakfast. I read a story out of the newspaper, "Children who do not eat breakfast do not do as well academically as their counterparts who *do* eat a good breakfast." He is unmoved, but condescends to drink one eggnog every morning. I press on and talk fiber. He is unimpressed. But maybe, he drawls in kid-like fashion, every once in a while he'll eat spaghetti, fish or leftovers for breakfast, BUT I'm not to tell any of his friends that I "feed" him "weird" food in the morning. We strike a deal.

As for lunch, well, could I deliver a McDonald's pizza to his classroom every day at 11:30?

Who would have thought that serving up a meal would be so exhausting? If there was one thing about rearing children that I thought would be easy, it was feeding them. I mean, it just seems so natural. Breathe, eat, grow—what's the problem?

Not one to take defeat lying down, I decided to investigate this picky-eater syndrome. Pad in hand I went begging for help. What I found were dozens, hundreds, dare I say thousands, of parents who are equally fed up with their children's eating habits. And it would seem that no one, not even the experts, is immune to the problem. I interviewed nutritionists who talked up a storm but, when the pad was closed and the pen put away, whispered, "*I* can't get my kids to eat a damn thing either. They're driving me crazy."

I spoke with child psychologists who gave all sorts of interesting insights. At the end of one interview a psychologist threw his hands in the air and said, "My son eats sausages and headcheese. Now tell me, how can anyone live on that?"

There's a lesson here: we're not alone.

We're not talking about eating disorders or food-related difficulties caused by emotional or physical problems. We're talking about little ones who use the word NO like a club, who won't sit still at the table, who turn up their noses at everything, who all-in-all are simply not following the "Perfect Family Meal" script!

1

SO, WHAT'S
A PICKY EATER?

Labeling a Picky Eater

First things first: The term "picky eater" is a "communicative term"—a way for one parent to talk to another parent or a professional about a situation that is causing the parent (seldom the child) grief. The term should not be directed to a child. Why? Because by labeling children "picky eaters" we may actually create picky eaters.

Children go through stages. At first they wolf down anything edible (and some things that aren't). Then one day they appear to stop eating altogether. They're not hungry. Seconds before the parents are about to trot them off to the doctor, they start eating again. Many a parent will notice a growth spurt at the end of this eat/pick/eat cycle. It also sometimes seems that small children somehow instinctively know when to eat and when not to eat. Some children, for example, appear to eat less in winter, while in the spring and fall they consume everything that isn't nailed down.

Now, if in the middle of these cycles, or seasons, we point to a child and say, "He's a picky eater," we may create a problem where none existed.

••

"My six-year-old daughter is an excellent eater and she tries different foods as well. One evening, after a long day at the beach, she simply didn't want to eat. My aunt announced, 'Oh look, you have a picky eater.' My daughter was embarrassed and tried to eat but ended up being sick. Labeling children can really offend them."

••

We all have different definitions of what a "picky eater" is. For example, a parent—call her Mary—may be a very plain cook. The household menu may not vary. Mary's young children will probably eat everything she cooks. However, they may not eat out or eat anything other people cook. Mary may not think of her children as picky eaters, but others would. Mary's children will eventually suffer the social problems all picky eaters have once they venture past their own kitchen door.

Are Your Child's Eating Habits a Problem?

Most children will refuse a couple of foods. A child who having tried a food, simply "doesn't like it," is exercising his or her rights. After all, we adults allow ourselves food preferences. I don't like canned peas. I don't know why I don't. I like pea soup. I like other kinds of legumes/peas/beans. I just don't like canned peas. And I am not going to eat them—so there! Does this make me a picky eater? No. It's the same with children. The child's whole diet, plus the dietary habits at home, must be taken into consideration before you decide that your child's picky eating is something to worry about.

Of course, there are some really good reasons why we should take a hard look at a picky-eater problem.

- A child who turns up her nose at most food creates friction at the table and in the house.
- Cooking a second meal before bedtime, or, worse, listening to a little voice call out at 2:00 am, "Mommy, I'm hungry" is both heart-rending and annoying.
- It's difficult to travel with a child who refuses to try new foods (or old foods for that matter).
- We live in a multicultural society. A child who eats only meat and potatoes, will eventually find himself left out. We make allowances for children who are picky eaters— as we should. But children grow. In most cases teenagers have grown out of the childhood anxiety about putting unfamiliar food in their mouths. They have a strong sense of control and are now able to let go and sample different foods. But those who maintain a hammerlock on their anxieties might find themselves at a serious social disadvantage both now and later on in life. Picture the up-and-coming business person declining to break bread with future clients because she "doesn't like their food."

· ·

"We invited a colleague and his wife over for dinner only to discover that he doesn't eat pasta, fish, salads, cooked vegetables, rice or anything with sauce on it. While his wife, my husband and I had a wonderful dinner, he ate hot dogs.

"He's really a nice guy, but unless we have a barbecue he won't be invited back in a hurry. And frankly, I'm a little afraid of eating at their home."

· ·

- The foremost concern in most parents' minds is that picky eating, carried on for a prolonged period, compromises a child nutritionally. After all, healthy eating and adequate nourishment are dependent on eating a variety of foods.

So let's assume for a moment that you are worried that your child's picky-eater behavior is compromising her health. Is she old enough to understand basic nutrition? Silly as this sounds, does your six-year-old know that she needs to eat certain foods to develop? The connection between food and health is not clear to all children. Most children have some airy-fairy ideas about carrots and X-ray vision, and spinach and muscles, but beyond that they are at a loss. Nutrition is taught in grades three or four in most public-school systems, but don't expect the school to teach your child about the intricacies. That's up to parents.

Beyond that, is your child really not getting enough fiber/calories/nutrients? Have you taken a good look at your child's total diet?

Realize that there is no such thing as a "bad" food. A bag of chips may not be our idea of a great snack, but one has to admit that there is some value in chips somewhere (although you may have to turn into an archeologist and dig about to find it). In fact, a small bag of chips will supply almost 20 percent of a four- to six-year-old's daily energy requirements. But wait—a bag of chips will not supply a child with 20 percent of his daily *nutritional* requirements.

In other words, chips are not the enemy, nor are they going to bring civilization as we know it to a grinding halt. (Don't for a second imagine I am suggesting a child eat processed chips as a rule.) Think about *all* the food your child consumes, not just the foods deemed "good for you."

Look at your child's food consumption from a weekly, not daily, perspective. It may even be necessary to take another step back and look at an even bigger picture—say over a few weeks. Remember that children go through growth spurts. From this vantage point many parents discover that their children are doing fine.

It's also common for parents not to notice little habits that prevent children from eating properly. Is she nipping into the Mom & Pop store on her way home from school? Does he trade off his lunch to the kid who comes to school laden with chocolate bars?

> "My babysitter would give my son a snack at 4:30. She eats dinner at 6:30, and I guess she thought we did too. But we eat as soon as I get home, around 5:00. No wonder my son never ate much at dinner."

Now take a hard look at the total family diet. Is there something the parent can do? Is there too much empty-calorie food in the house? Are there examples being set in the home that are counter to everything being said and taught? Do Mom and Dad have radically different views of what good eating is about? (A child may actually eat what Daddy eats to prove to that parent that she loves him best. If Daddy eats bags of chips half the night in front of the TV, a precedent is being set.)

It may be necessary to keep a diary of your child's food habits, but remember—if too much attention is focused on the problem, if a parent becomes obsessed with the child's eating habits, or if the child feels pressured, a small problem might balloon into a large one.

Talk to the doctor. Hit the books. Call up the local health unit and ask to speak to a nutritionist. Explore. If a child is fit, both physically and emotionally, she will not starve.

Role Models

Most of what is written and said about picky eaters focuses on the child. After all, it's the child who won't eat, therefore it's the child who must be "fixed." Not necessarily. How do you feel when your child refuses to eat? Frustrated? Angry? Challenged? Out of control?

It's unnerving to see one's child change from a little soul who eats like a horse (between six months and one year) turn into a picky eater (anytime after one year). To some parents a child's refusal of food feels like a direct challenge to their authority. A parent may overreact and attempt to force a child to eat, and in the end put undue emphasis on an issue that was not a problem—but will soon become one.

If a child is picking at her food to get attention, then a parent who gets upset is delivering that (negative) attention. Completely ignore the child's behavior. Remove her plate with the rest of the family's plates and carry on as if nothing has happened. REMEMBER, and repeat this to yourself, IF YOUR CHILD IS HEALTHY, SHE WILL NOT STARVE.

What examples are you giving your children that might give them a dislike of food? For example, one parent might constantly berate herself for being "too fat." The parent who treats food like the enemy may be sending out the message that food is "bad."

Most North Americans have a running battle with food. We don't like our bodies. It should come as no surprise to see that the up-and-coming generation suffers from a variety of until-now almost unheard-of diet related ailments—anorexia nervosa and bulimia are examples. Every effort must be made not to have the next generation take up arms.

Another parent may say, jokingly, that she would never, oh yuck, try sushi. The message here is that it's OK, even good, to dislike some food. Children do divide up the world (and food) into categories, namely, good and bad.

Experiment. Laugh. It's OK not to like a specific food but it's not OK to voice an opinion about foods without having tried them. Think of the words we use to children, "Just *try* it," we sing (harp?) over and over again. Exemplify the "trying." Head out to different restaurants and learn what there is to learn. Watch the unspoken signals, the body signals that every child reads from birth—a wrinkled nose, crossed arms, a chair pushed back from the table, a funny sniff, a silly face. (Yes, I am talking about *adult* behavior here.)

Some parents nibble all day long and pick at dinner. Children need to eat frequently during the day. However, when a child picks at her meal, a parent can become annoyed. Why, when the child is just copying parent?

Before you say another word about your child's eating habits, spend a day and record—that is to say, *write down*—every morsel of food and drink that passes your lips. List the times and places. (Pretty scary, huh!) You may be surprised to discover that your children are following a similar eating pattern.

How we eat, what we eat, how much or how little we eat, when and where we eat, and how we appreciate the food from other cultures, all help to define our values as individuals and as a culture. These are the values that we want to pass on to our children. We can't force them to try different foods. The best we can do is to provide them with excellent examples, encouragement, and a never-ending array of foods to sample. Keep it all in perspective. What may be refused one day, may be sampled another day and gobbled up on the third day. Rush it, push it, demand it—and we'll turn a picky eater into a defiant little person.

Signs of Inadequate Nutrition

A child's body is a well-designed little machine; it can run on determination for quite some time. Often it's not the body that will tip off a parent to a child's poor nourishment; rather it's the child's behavior.

A child who is sleepy at 9:30 in the morning is either going to bed too late or not eating a proper breakfast. Perhaps it's a little of both.

There are many reasons why a child may be docile, inattentive, aggressive or unresponsive. An inadequate diet may be only one of those reasons. A behavior change should be brought to the attention of your child's doctor and caretaker.

A child who is well-nourished and otherwise healthy will:

- Have shiny hair, pink gums and good teeth.
- Sleep well under normal conditions.
- Not tire easily.
- Be alert and energetic.
- Have good muscle control, tone and posture.
- On most occasions have a good appetite and good elimination.
- Have healthy-colored skin with a smooth texture.

In spite of all that, a child who is drinking a great deal of milk, for example, may have shiny hair, pink gums, and so on, and yet still be undernourished. Again, the total diet must be considered.

A child who is not eating at all, or deliberately avoiding food, is not a picky eater. He or she is a child in distress and needs professional attention. In some cases, there may be a physical reason—the child may be ill. In other cases, the child may be dealing with an emotional problem. Refusing food is one way of crying out for help without actually verbalizing the problem.

Note: If your baby is under one year and displays *any* of these signs, don't wait for your doctor to return your call. Take your baby to the hospital.

Why Children Don't Eat

Child development and parenting are interwoven with a child's dietary habits. Before you identify your child as a picky eater who needs to change, realize that a child who refuses to eat does so for a reason. Some of the reasons are perfectly acceptable. Some of the reasons need to be looked into, and others can be ignored, as they will pass.

Young children don't eat because:
• They are sick, tired, bored or listless.
• They are full.
• They don't need as much food as we think they do.
• It is their right to say no.
• They are more interested in talking than eating.
• They are not in a growth spurt and aren't really hungry.
• They are ticked off and want you to know it.
• They need attention, and refusing food is one way to get it.
• They feel that they haven't any control over their lives and want to assert themselves.
• Something has gone wrong in their lives and they don't know how to express themselves.
• The flavor is too overpowering, or instinct (sniff, sniff) tells them that the food "isn't right."
• Meals are associated with threats, bribes, nagging, coaxing and yelling.

A child who is being run ragged might want to cry "halt," and use food to do it. And if refusing to eat will send Mom round the bend, then why not use that to get attention? (Negative attention is, as we well know, better than no attention at all.)

Call the Doctor If:

- Your infant has refused two feedings in a row.
- Your baby/child shows signs of dehydration (no wet diapers after ten hours, no tears, a sticky or gummy mouth, sunken eyes, pasty or baggy skin).
- Your child has severe cramps and/or a bloated tummy.
- Your child is listless, confused, disorientated or lethargic.
- Your child complains of a headache and/or blurred vision.
- Your child is persistently vomiting, or is vomiting and has a fever.
- Over a period of forty-eight hours, your baby/child has runny stools or is constipated. (The time period here varies, depending on age. When in doubt, act.)
- There is blood in your child's stools, or the stools are very black and tar-like.
- You have that certain, indescribable feeling that something is wrong with your child.
- Your child withdraws from the social scene, refuses food and/or becomes hostile, depressed or sullen.

Natural Consequences

Hunger is the natural consequence of not eating. A parent might say to a child, "This is your lunch. Eat what you want, but there will be nothing else served until your snack at 3 o'clock."

Before trying this tactic, stop and think. From a child's point of view, how far away is 3 o'clock? Is that tonight? Tomorrow? Children cotton on to the concept of time at different stages. Because of the often-rigid schedules kept, a child who attends daycare often has a good grasp of how long one or two hours actually is. Use your own judgment.

Comfort Food

To encourage a child to try new foods, never force, bribe or pander. Recognize the connection between food and love, love and food. Nursing a baby may be the most wonderful and obvious way we show our love for our baby. The connection between comfort, caring and all good things is apparent to an hour-old infant. The connection can still be apparent to the six-, ten-, or twelve-year-old. Notice, too, that the connection between food and caring is not based on dependence.

It's totally acceptable to provide comfort with a soothing glass of hot chocolate. It's not acceptable to depend on food to solve problems. A parent might want to talk to a specialist if he/she suspects that a child is depending on food for emotional support.

Keep in mind, too, that children have very small tummies. It's not unusual for a child to eat ten or more times a day. Children simply can't be expected to eat large meals at one sitting.

Many parents will say, "If you don't eat your dinner you'll get no dessert." Pity. Dessert should not be a reward for eating. And since many people have switched from the heavy, cream-laden desserts of times past to fresh fruit and cheese, desserts now play a nutritional role in a child's diet.

Realistic Expectations

As soon as they are able, we want our children to begin to *take control* of their behavior and eventually be *responsible* for it. (Easier said than done.) What can we expect from a child? Should we expect a three-year-old to say no to Grandpa's handout of a bag of candies? Would we expect a ten-year-old to say no to a second bag of chips?

Probably not.

Let's be realistic here so that we don't aggravate a piddling problem ("I don't wanna eat that") and perhaps change it into a show-stopping crisis ("I won't eat that—ever").

Don't ever expect a child not to eat a yummy cookie if it's sitting within sight and reach or handed to him on a silver platter. Nor should we expect a child to gobble up a serving of carrots just because *we* consider them to be "good-for-you" food.

Turn the tables. Imagine. You're lying in bed. In the fridge is a plate full of _____ (insert your favorite treat here). You know you shouldn't eat just before bed. You could be grown-up about it, roll over and go to sleep. Or, you could rub your hands in glee, slip your tootsies into your slippers and pitter-patter down to the fridge for a snack. Hey, Dagwood Bumstead does it all the time. Do you think Dagwood ever snuck down the stairs for a plate of yummy lima beans? (Mind you, Dagwood hasn't put on a pound in decades!)

Remember, what we want eventually is a child who is *responsible* for his own food intake. A child who is merely *obedient* might eat everything in front of him, not because he's hungry, but because he wants approval. An obedient child who obeys adults without question all the time may, among other things, find himself vulnerable to every dietary fad imaginable and may never take control of his own food intake.

Obedient children often have not had the opportunity to find out who they really are. Oh, it's nice to be the mom of the best-behaved child in the school, the one who gets the award for being Miss Sweetness-and-Light, but in the long run the child who has struck out on her own, who has tested the waters, is the one who is most prepared to try new things—and new foods.

Again, a child dubbed a picky eater may simply be asserting herself—taking control. To demand that this child, at this stage of development, eat everything put in front of her is to start a war that no one can win and everyone may lose. Only a parent can make the distinction between a child who is asserting his or her rights and a child who is a picky eater. As a rule of thumb, picky eaters are suspicious of most food. A child who is asserting his or her rights will usually (but not always) take a stand for a short period of time. If this stand is acknowledged and the situation rectified to everyone's satisfaction, the child will resume normal eating habits.

....

"Sarah always behaved well and ate whatever was put in front of her. Her older sister, Ruthie, constantly challenged us. Oh, she tried food all right, but only when the mood struck her. We felt Ruthie was a picky eater. Ruthie is now in college. She eats all sorts of exotic foods and cooks everything under the sun. She's a healthy weight. Sarah eats what everyone else eats. In her high-school years she ate every afternoon at a local fast-food restaurant with her friends. Last year she lived with a roommate who was a vegetarian, and so she became a vegetarian. Now she lives with a girl who we think is anorexic. All Sarah now eats is diet food. It strikes me that Sarah was never encouraged to be responsible in many areas of her life, and at the moment this lack of responsibility is reflected in her eating habits."

....

Goals

Our goal? Certainly it's not to *feed* our children—"feeding" being more suitable for farm animals. Nor is it appropriate to beg, bribe or pander to children's outlandish requests.

Our goal is to charm our children—to intrigue them. Just as we hope to tweak their interests in science and art, the plan is to calm their anxieties and allow them to see food as nourishment, as a continuation of their cultural heritage (e.g., a kosher diet), and as a means of approaching a new culture. And of course, we want them to enjoy the whole experience.

There's more.

All parents want their children to learn to make sensible decisions. Those decisions, we hope, will extend to their choice and consumption of food. We want them to eat food that's good, safe and tasty. And we want them to know when to stop eating. That means that, hard as it may appear, we must never push food into children (that is, "feed" them). To stuff a child past her limit is to teach her to ignore her own inner voice.

Likewise, the parent who stops a child from eating *good* food ("You've had enough") also attempts to control a child's appetite.

The Fat Farce

Remember the 1980s and the Big Sugar Scare? It seemed that everywhere we looked we were being told to hold the sugar. As it turns out, sugar isn't all that evil after all. True, we don't need it and it's a good idea to reduce the sugar in our children's overall diet, but it's not the major health concern we were told it was. But now we're in the 90s and we have the Fat Scare. Yes, it would appear that the evil fat lurking in our food is gonna get us. Hang on. Adults should reduce the amount of fat in their total diet, but parents *must not* eliminate fat from a child's diet. About 40 to 50 percent of the energy spent by a baby and toddler should come from fat. Children over two years of age should have a diet composed of 30 to 35 percent fat.

What goal do we want our children to have for themselves? What goal do *we* have for our children? In both cases the answer should be: health. We want our children to maintain a healthy weight in relation to their body size. Unfortunately, too many parents see baby's protruding tummy as being a sign of future weight problems. More than one parent has overreacted by putting a chubby infant on a diet. Don't ever do that!

Deep-six labels such as "fatty," "skinny," "chubby" and, of course, "picky eater." They don't do any good but can do great harm.

In General—What Works

Many problems, food-related and otherwise, are tied to children's emotional swings. A child who is anxious about an upcoming school play may not eat because he's nervous. A child who has been bullied that day may not eat because she's upset. Tips, tricks, and innovative recipes will not entice any child into eating if the reason for not eating is emotional.

That said, there are four points which are crucial to developing the dietary and culinary world of the child:

(1) Present food in a way that shows your love. (Whoa, we're not talking about preparing a smoked-salmon mousse for lunch.) Let's say your child loves apples. If he likes apples whole, fine. But an apple thinly sliced and "designed" on a little plate says, "I did this for you because I know you like it this way."

Or, what would it mean to a child if you came home with the type of cereal that only she likes? Such a gesture recognizes that the child is different from her siblings, and acknowledges the link between caring and food.

(2) Separate yourself from your child's rejection. Picture this: you design a landscape with broccoli and asparagus,

potatoes and cheese. (See page 115 for recipe.) What a masterpiece! Your child looks at it, says "yuck" and shrugs. It's in the nature of the young child to be self-centered. Without belaboring the point or imposing guilt—tell your child how his comment made you feel ("Andrew, that hurt my feelings"). But don't take it personally, and don't force your child to eat a meal simply because you have invested time in preparing it.

• •

Murphy's mom must have said it. "The more time you spend preparing a meal, the less likely is your child to eat it."

• •

(3) Don't try to get your child to eat. Chances are, the more you try, the less likely you are to succeed.

(4) Be realistic. Some children just don't eat very much, yet thrive beautifully. Understand the nature of your child's appetite. Some children are "grazers"—they eat in little spurts. Other children will eat more readily if they have exercised before dinner.

• •

"We had a set routine. We'd pick the kids up at the babysitter's. I'd start dinner immediately after we arrived home, while the girls did their homework. They would hardly touch their food. I thought I was saddled with two very picky eaters. My husband started running after we got home, and since I decided to go with him the girls joined us on their bikes! What a difference. Their appetites improved enormously. Frankly, I wonder if a lot of kids appear to be picky eaters but in fact just don't get enough exercise."

• •

• •

It's a parent's job to provide children with an array of good, nutrient-dense foods. It's a child's right to choose what to eat.

• •

The Myth

It's been said that if you offer children a variety of foods they will intuitively eat what's good for them. Oh *please*! Given the choice between a donut and a celery stick, the vast majority of children will pick the donut—as will most adults, come to think of it.

The idea that good nutrition is somehow instinctive or guided by some inner light, may have come from an experiment done by Clara Davis in 1930. In Davis's experiment, orphaned children were confined to a room and given an array of foods to eat. The children grew well. It was surmised that if given choices children would pick appropriate food. The hitch was that all the food offered the children in this experiment was natural and what we would define as "good-for-you" foods. Heck, there wasn't a jelly donut in sight.

Children are people too, and it's the rare, although not unheard-of, child who won't opt for the tasty and the sweet. That having been said, it should also be noted that the internal instincts of a child are a lot sharper than those of an adult. They do know *what* appeals to them, *when* they are hungry and *when* they should stop eating.

2

RIGHT FROM
THE START

Baby

We can make an effort to discourage (though we can never eliminate) picky-eating tendencies by tackling the potential problem right at the beginning. Breast is best, naturally. Hopefully, baby has been fed on demand and already connects nurture with food. However, once solid food is introduced a parent can go a long way in showing respect for a child by not insisting that the baby eat positively everything. It's even worse to measure out a child's food in accordance with some goof-ball theory that says baby should eat X number of ounces and that's it. A baby will eat until she's full—period. Trust your babe to know the difference between full and hungry.

Tips

- Commercially prepared infant cereals are designed for a baby's digestive system. They're fortified with a highly absorbable form of iron, enriched with calcium, phosphorus and vitamins B1 and B2 and niacin. They're a good buy.

Start off with a single-grain cereal such as rice. Introduce only one cereal at a time (introduce a new grain once a week) and watch for an allergic reaction. One tablespoon per meal for the first few days is enough. Once your baby adjusts to the new sensation he'll more than make up for lost time.

- Commercially prepared baby food is excellent. Long gone are the days when food manufacturers added salt. But, you will find sugar in very few dessert items—check the list of ingredients on the jar. However, commercially prepared baby food is expensive. If you're like most families you'll make some of your own food and supplement it with store-bought food. (Keep those baby-food jars. Sterilize them and use them for your homemade baby food.)

- Don't delay too long before introducing different textures. In most cases (which may not include your child's case) a baby is introduced to strained (pureed) food around five to six months. Next comes mashed (lumpy-soft) around six to seven months. Minced food (very lumpy) is introduced around seven to nine months, followed by chopped at nine to twelve months, and cut up at twelve to eighteen months. Having said all that, I might also mention that both my sons lagged behind this rather rigid schedule with no adverse effects. (At least neither of them is taking up arms or showing pathological tendencies—yet.)

- Egg yolks can be introduced after six months, but since egg whites have been known to cause allergic reactions in some babies, nix the whites until after twelve months.

- There is no unequivocal evidence (yet) that all preservatives are harmful. However, salt and fat are present in excess in many preserved meats. Avoid wieners, bacon, sausages and many prepared meats.

- To give babies the comfort of a familiar taste, mix vegetables with a little formula.
- The Canadian Paediatric Society recommends that you give a baby fluoride supplements at around six months of age if the water where you live is not fluoridated. (Formula mixed with fluoridated water will give your baby enough fluoride.)

True, delaying the introduction of solids too long is not a good idea, but neither is rushing the process, or thinking that a child's intelligence rests on her ability to eat a chopped banana. Talk to your child's doctor before starting her on solids, and keep in mind that what's good for your neighbor's child is not necessarily right for your child. And remember, while some babies/children develop food-related anxieties for reasons known only to Martians, most won't if they have had good experiences with food all along.

••

WARNING! Discourage older siblings from giving their food to baby brother or sister. (Food eaten by older children may choke a baby.) This can be very confusing for big brothers and sisters who are being told to "share" all the time.

••

- Introduce vegetables first. There's no nutritional benefit, but fruits are sweet and very appealing. It may be hard to convince babies to enjoy vegetables with the same gusto.
- Avoid using butter, margarine, salt, excess pepper, spices, herbs or added sweeteners during the baby's first year.
- Buy a food processor or blender. Don't put too much in the blender at one time—$^3/_4$ cup (175 ml) is

enough—otherwise the food will have mixed textures. (Test it by rubbing a sample between two fingers. If it's grainy give it another whirl.)

- Buy a really good steamer and a baby-food grinder. (The grinder can be used for grinding nuts and such after baby has moved on to steak.)
- Do not toss canned food designed for adults into the blender. The sodium and sugar content are usually too high for a baby. Stick to processing fresh or home-cooked foods.
- Use plain yogurt to thicken hot cereals.
- Add your own fruit to plain yogurt.
- Mix mashed cottage cheese or tofu with a favorite mashed fruit.

....

Avocados can be considered "perfect" baby food. They mash well with other foods such as tofu, and contain a variety of vitamins and nutrients and necessary fats. As baby grows, avocados can be sliced and served as first finger-foods.

....

- Purists would suggest that a parent avoid commercial ice cream altogether since it's high in sugar. However, there's more to life than a strict adherence to nutrition. And what would a first birthday party be without ice cream? There are many varieties of ice cream. Spend a moment in the freezer department and read the labels. Try frozen yogurt as an alternative. Again, read the labels, as this product also contains sugar. Tasting hot/cold is a tactile experience. By all means let baby experiment. (Get the reactions on video.)
- Freeze homemade baby food in sterilized ice-cube trays. When frozen, pop them out of the tray and seal in a freezer bag. Take one out as needed and defrost. Or, plop

tablespoons of food on a small cookie sheet or a piece of waxed paper. Freeze and wrap accordingly. Label and date the food. Keep for not more than two months. (Never refreeze food that has thawed.)

- She's a mess. Cereal is all over her face, in her hair, ears, down her shirt—the bib is clean, though! Try not to mop baby up after each bite. Feeding a baby is not meant to be a tidy exercise. Most children do not like having their faces wiped with a facecloth. Since the plan is to establish respect for the child, and a pleasant mealtime atmosphere, try not to swoop down on an unsuspecting child with a wet cloth. Either hand over the cloth and let your child make her best effort, wipe baby's face with your own wet hands (preferred to the dreaded cloth by most babies, for some strange reason) or give her a little bowl of water and let her dip her own fingers in along with yours.

"I thought I would remember everything—like, Eli had his first mouthful of peas on Wednesday morning, his first taste of lamb on Friday morning and so on. Well, he did break out in a rash, and for the life of me I couldn't remember which day he ate what. Now that Sarah has come along I introduce a new food every Monday and write it down on the kitchen calendar."

- Vary the menu. Yes, babies do have taste buds—and very sensitive ones at that. If baby is to grow into a toddler who will enjoy new foods, then start the taste-testing process early.
- No means "no." Do not force-feed a child. Respect for a child begins here.
- Wielding a spoon is great fun. Give her a spoon and bowl of her own. If necessary feed her from another bowl.

- Buy a highchair with as few bells and whistles as possible. Who needs a highchair that reclines? Children should not be given solid food while lying down—ever! And the fewer the gadgets, the less likely it is that food will be caught in crevices.
- A good tray on a highchair is solid and wide (to play with Play-Doh, crayons and bang with a spoon). Trays that can be lifted or moved with one hand are also best.
- Stand a highchair in the shower for a good cleaning or hose it down outside. Let it dry in the sun.

Toddlers (One-Year-Olds)

This is it, your window into your child's culinary future. Most children will willingly sample new foods between their first and second year. Now is the time to have fun. Your child will nibble on salty capers, actually eat smoked salmon, dip his shrimp and giggle at smoked oysters. It's as important to introduce new textures at this stage as it is new tastes. (Chewing ability varies at this stage. Offer children tiny "tastes" of this and that and, as always, watch for any signs of allergic reaction.)

The pity here is that many parents will decide that small children will not "appreciate" expensive or exotic food. Since children's willingness to sample the new and strange magically disappears by the time they reach the school years, their appreciation of unusual foods may never appear—or at least, not nearly so readily.

A lot of growing takes place between the first and second birthdays. In terms of ages and stages, one could almost divide the year up by months. A twelve-month-old for example, is as likely to shovel her peas into her ear as into her mouth. (It's not that she doesn't know that they're supposed to go in her mouth, it's that the one-year-old may be determined to use a spoon and damn the torpedoes.)

"Me do it," is the demand of the day, and just try—go on, try—to offer a helping hand. Ha!

It's also around this time that toddlers learn the difference between food and other objects. For example, toddlers spend an inordinate amount of time tossing toys and such onto the floor and demanding their return. Mom and Daddy, in retriever fashion, step and fetch. But now something is amiss. When toddler tosses her carrots on the floor, they are not returned. Hey, wait a minute—they're put in the garbage! Why? The difference between food and other substances begins to emerge.

Toddlers don't necessarily connect tasting with swallowing. Food is a total tactile experience. Like small animals, children will touch (poke, mush, smash, crush and toss) their food. Then, and only then, may it be sniffed and put into the mouth. Out it may come again. This child is not a picky eater. This behavior is programed, and a parent obsessed with keeping the eating process "clean" may well hamper this normal exploratory activity.

••

"I remember watching my grandmother feed my baby brother. She always held the bowl and would mop him up after each mouthful. During feeding time he was dressed from head to toe in plastic. If he spat his food back out he was called a 'dirty boy.' My granny was wonderful to us, but she grew up in a time when washing machines and dryers didn't exist. Cleanliness was almost everything."

••

Expect an almost sudden (at least it will appear that way) drop in a baby's appetite after her first birthday. First-time parents will find this stage unnerving. You're in good company. Support services for new parents state that they receive a flood of calls from new parents concerning a baby's food intake when the baby is between fifteen and twenty-eight months.

How much food does a toddler need per meal? As much as she wants. Or, taking age and weight into consideration, she needs a dollop of this, a tiny bit of that and a smidgen of those. (Some experts have suggested that a basic rule of thumb should be: one tablespoon from each food group per meal for each year of life. Other experts have called such a rule "dumb." Start with one tablespoon per food group and work from there according to your child's needs.)

Balance and variety are usually more important than quantity. Besides, if a toddler continued to eat with the same voracity as the eight- or nine-month-old baby, she'd weigh-in at a hefty couple of tons by her tenth birthday.

If your child is growing normally, and is alert and happy, you can be sure he's getting enough to eat.

••

WARNING! It's possible to suppress a toddler/child's appetite with too much juice or milk. A toddler, generally speaking, should have 4 ounces (125 g) of juice a day. Mix the 4 ounces with equal parts of water to make up 8 ounces (250 g). Naturally, a child will require more water and/or juice on a hot day. Avoid giving toddlers and children milk within an hour or so of a meal.

••

Tips
- Peel or clean carrots and slit lengthwise to reduce (though it will not eliminate) the chance of choking. Steam them until they can easily be broken with a pinch of the fingers. Do not give a raw, uncooked carrot

27

to a child under three. (Remember to stay with your child at all times during his meal.)

- Peanut butter spread on white bread can "ball-up" in the throat and cause a child to choke. Hot dogs can be a problem too. If you serve them to small children, slit them in half lengthwise. Grapes, nuts, carrots, many raw vegetables and popcorn can also cause problems. Slice bananas lengthwise. Always teach a child to sit up when eating and never, never let a child, young or old, lie in front of the TV and eat.

- It's a matter of personal opinion, but most child-care experts suggest that baby should not be weaned off the bottle too suddenly. With new tastes to savor and a new world to discover, it's nice to have a friendly ol' bottle around to provide comfort. Not all "comfort" bottles need to be milk—water or diluted juice will suffice. Watch your child's teeth closly, however. If your child is still on the bottle after a year and a half, you may want to start regular dental checkups.

- Toddlers do not need vitamin supplements if they are eating a variety of foods. Overloading a child's body with vitamins can cause problems. If you feel that your toddler needs vitamins, talk to your child's doctor.

- Choice at this age can be confusing, even overwhelming. It's often best to put two foods (carrots and bits of chicken, for example) on her plate first and, after they are eaten, add the potatoes and whatever.

Vitamin pills, particularly the chewable kind, are not only tasty, but because of the variety of shapes they come in, are very appealing to toddlers. Iron-fortified vitamin pills, taken in quantity, can cause great harm. Treat vitamins like medicine: keep them out of sight and reach in a locked cabinet, and never refer to them as candy.

Toddlers Plus (Two-Year-Olds)

He takes forever to walk a block, and even longer to eat a spoonful of peas. Once in a while he'll let you feed him, but on the whole he'll manage himself, thanks.

It's around this age that a child may begin to declare herself a picky eater. ("No, no, no. Don't want it.") It's also around this stage that parents introduce the threat as a means of getting the child to eat. Example: "Eat your lunch or you'll get nothing else until dinner."

THE THREAT

Time-threats ("No TV tonight unless you eat") do not work with the two-year-old simply because, living in the immediate present, she can't think past the next minute, let alone several hours. She also doesn't have any sense of time. The next meal may be next month for all she knows or cares. Besides, "eat or I'll put you in your room" has some rather sticky and undesirable results. Soon she'll start to connect her room, or going to bed, with punishment. Since sleeping problems are the second most common concern of the parents of children in this age group (after food and before potty concerns), it's a threat to be avoided.

All threats should be avoided. In the long run they don't work, and they set a parenting style that's hard to break.

HERE COMES THE BRIBE

"Eat your peas and you'll get a treat/dessert." Or, "If you don't eat your broccoli you won't get a treat/dessert." Ah, the bribe.
There's no denying it, bribing a child to eat can get positive results—at least in the short term. The problem with bribery, over the long haul, is that children will come to expect a reward for desired behavior. "What, no treat for eating the salad? Well, why should I eat the salad?" may be a young child's thinking.

We've all bribed children at some point. (Remember the last time you were in a restaurant with your four-year-old. Now what did you whisper to her to get her to come out from under the table?) The problem, again, is that if bribery is used a lot, a pattern will be established that will become difficult to break.

Not that bribes always work. Despite the fact that it's considered politically incorrect to refer to the two-year-old as being in the "terrible twos" (now replaced by the phrase "terrific twos"), a two-year-old by any name is an obstinate little fellow. He must be, he has a personality to develop. And when a bribe is offered it's in the nature of the two-year-old to say no. He might want to say yes, but he'll say no anyway. Therefore the taste of the food may not be an issue at all. The child simply says no because he needs to hear himself say no.

....

"The only green thing my son would eat was mint ice cream."
....

COAXING AND NAGGING

"Come on, open up. That's my good girl. Open up for Mommy/Daddy/Granny. Here comes the airplane. Look, Mommy likes the stewed prunes. Ummmmmm, good."

This can go on for some time. What fun it must be to sit in the highchair and watch everyone at the table making complete idiots of themselves. Has anyone ever had any success with this one?

....

"We're thrilled with our daughter's choice of profession—she's going to be an engineer. She's four, and already developing irrigation techniques with her mashed potatoes. We have never seen her actually eat the potatoes, however."
....

Tips

- The brighter the better. Carrots, strawberries, green, orange and red peppers, oranges and tomatoes are all delightful to look at and play with. Eventually they will be taste-tested too. Serve the vegetables and fruits raw with a yogurt-based dip. (Take a favorite package of dried, prepared salad dressing and mix with plain yogurt.)

- Some vegetables may go uneaten. It's better to let them remain untouched than quickly to substitute a favored vegetable. Children should not come to expect that their rejection of one food will result in their getting a preferred food.

- Spread infant meat baby food on bread or crackers and serve as a sandwich. Most toddlers will recognize the familiar taste of infant meat, and you'll have the satisfaction of knowing that they're getting a very healthy sandwich.

- Ask your two-and-a-half-year-old for her "opinion" about dinner. Help her with the descriptive words such as delicious, yummy, tasty, not very good, and so on. In order to give you an opinion she'll have to taste it. Respect that opinion.

- By all means take your child out to a family restaurant for a meal. However, it's totally unrealistic to expect a two- to four-year-old to eat "properly" or to behave during a meal out. Go out to dinner prepared with a bag of tricks—crayons, small cars and so on. You may even want to bring a "snack"—food is never delivered fast enough for a toddler.

- Give your toddler empty cereal boxes to play with. Familiarity does not breed contempt. The more she's used to the look of the boxes different foods come in, the more likely she will be to taste-test the contents.

- Put a few chosen snacks in a plastic container and let her pick and choose her own snack at will.

Little Boys and Little Girls
(Three- and Four-Year-Olds)

He's three and he's a man—in charge of his own destiny, in command. A force to be reckoned with. He can dress himself (sort of), he can play with a friend without smacking him (some of the time), he can wield utensils (after a fashion) and he can be an absolute pleasure to be around (most of the time).

That's not all.

Children over three have a tenuous grasp of the concept of time. If your little boy or girl uses the drag-it-out-until-Mom-gets-fed-up technique to avoid eating, now would be a good time to set a timer. Decide how long a meal should take to eat—say, twenty minutes or so. (Keep in mind that most children's attention span is pushed to the limit after twenty minutes.) Explain to your child that after twenty minutes, or when the timer goes off, her plate will be taken away. Make sure your child can see the timer. In the beginning remind her once or twice that time is passing. Remove the plate without fanfare and let her run off and play. Don't get caught in the "just five more minutes" trap. Be nice. The point is to allow natural consequences to kick in and let your child experience hunger. Be sure to tell your child that snack time is not too far away. (Let's not be mean about this.)

Habits and Routines

Some of the habits and routines children develop can drive a parent batty.

- "If there were four different items on her plate she'd demand four different forks."
- "He wouldn't eat his potatoes if they 'touched' his meat."

- "She'd only drink out of the glass with the cow painted on it. I ended up carrying it around with me."

Routines such as these, harmless unless taken to extremes, help a child center himself. They are familiar, comforting. They also demand that others take note. They say, "Look at me, I'm important." These little rituals tend to pass quickly because they take a lot of effort on a child's part. Problems can arise if a parent confronts these harmless rituals with common sense!

• •

"My husband simply couldn't understand why our daughter would eat only one item on her plate at a time. She'd eat up all of her meat, then all of her vegetables, then all of her potatoes and so on. She'd make a little play out of it. Her father would constantly say to her, 'Have a bit of meat and then potato and then carrots.' I think my husband thought she was doing this to irritate him and you know, after a long time, I think she *was* doing it because it bugged him. It didn't start out that way, though."

• •

Rituals pass if tolerated with a little humor. If these rituals become compulsions and stick around for many months, talk to your doctor.

Tips
- Avoid showing anxiety about which foods are eaten and which ones are not. For example, a parent may insist that a child eat her vegetables and ignore the meat, or vice versa. Children pick up on these inconsistencies.
- At a restaurant a child may sample a food that she rejected at home.

33

- Three- to five-year-olds still find the wielding of utensils a little tiring. Occasionally give them permission to use their fingers.
- The more often a child sees a particular food, the more likely she will be to try it. If, for example, she doesn't like rice, acknowledge it, but put a tiny bit of it on her plate anyway. (Be nice about it.) She doesn't have to eat it, just look at it.
- Try out new recipes and ask your child to taste-test them in the kitchen. In your most serious tone ask, "Do you think I've added enough pepper?" or "Do you think Mommy/Daddy will like this?" Because the food has not been presented at the table, most children are much more apt to taste and comment. (This exercise also works well with school-age children.)
- Use your playgroup as a recipe-tasting forum. Children always want a snack mid-morning and will often try a food that their buddy is munching on. This is also a great time to introduce different tastes or spices from other cultures. If you or your grandparents are from a different culture and have recipes from that culture, do try a few out on the group.
- It's fun for a child to be spoon-fed and play "baby" once in a while, especially if there is a new infant in the house. It's not appropriate to spoon-feed a child with the intent of shoveling the food into her.
- Serve new foods alongside familiar foods to minimize the shock.

••

"The only beans my son eats are jelly beans."

••

Small Scholars (Five Plus)

Say the words "peer pressure" to a parent. What's the reaction? Right. A curled lip. Wait, peer pressure can be very positive. If your child hooks up with a child who *will* try new foods, you're in luck!

No matter how much social savvy your new scholar has, she'll now succumb to peer pressure. Peers, for example, will usually dictate the type of lunchbox to carry. And peers may also dictate what type of food should go into those boxes. This can be annoying, but most children, if allowed to follow the pack on such harmless issues, will usually feel more comfortable at school. Eventually she'll break away from the pack, particularly if she discovers that she doesn't actually *like* what the other kids are eating.

••

Quick tip: Brown-bag it during the first two or so weeks of school and *then* take your child out to buy a lunchbox. Why? One wouldn't want to be stuck with a lunchbox that carries the "wrong" (that is, out-of-date) cartoon character on the front. Heaven forbid! Chances are you'll save yourself some money if you wait until your child tells you which lunchbox to buy.

••

A parent's tenuous control over a child's food consumption may seem as if it's slipped entirely once the child is off to school. Not so. The children really are watching. Parents are examples—no news there. But, turn up your nose at certain foods, and not only will your child do so too, she'll likely extend the snub to other foods.

Then there are the food jags popular with most school-age kids, preteens and teens. Think back—you'll probably remember your own childhood food preferences.

Food jags, by lay definition are a child's craving for just one or two types of food over a period of time. (I once ate chicken fried rice for lunch for an entire year. My long-suffering Mom fried it up and put it in a wide-mouth thermos every morning. To date I've shown no adverse effects, and I still like chicken fried rice.)

Food jags are normal and, many would say, a child's way of asserting his or her own personality.

Look at it this way. What can children control? They didn't want a little brother, but they got one anyway. And they don't own anything. Oh sure, Mom says Amanda owns her clothes—then how come they ended up on cousin Nicky's back just 'cause they were too small? And they don't own their toys, 'cause if they did they certainly wouldn't share them with the kid next door. Nope, they don't own anything, and they don't control much EXCEPT when and where they go to the potty, when (if?) they go to sleep and what they eat.

••

"Clean your plate" is a phrase that's had its day. "Eat until you're full and no between-meal snacks" is a better saying.

••

Tips

- Ask your picky eaters to write a list of all their favorite foods. You may be surprised to see just how many foods they *do* like. Together, divide the list of foods into the different food groups. Your children will now notice where they are coming up short. You may also want to try to include some of the foods in the less-favored groups at different meals.

- Now is the time to buy your child his own cookbook. If this is his first cookbook, make sure that it is very easy to read and follow. It's often better to buy a too-easy book then a book to grow into. The more success in the beginning, the better. The book should be a hardcover, and when pressed down, should lie flat on the table. (Spiral-bound books work well.) Cookbooks that illustrate each step and show which utensils are needed, are terrific.

- Write out in block letters a recipe your child can "read" himself. (Draw pictures, too.) Encourage your child to make a meal from the recipe.
- If space in the kitchen allows, give each child a different shelf (or divide one small shelf) for his or her goodies. Why? This idea will save you from discovering stashes of month-old chips under beds—best identified by the legions of ants marching down the hall.

It's not uncommon for children to stash food in their bedrooms, especially if there's a pesky smaller sibling around who has a habit of eating favored and savored treats. Hiding and hoarding food is something else again, and may point to a deeper problem. Some young children will hoard food because they fear going hungry, because they feel guilty about being hungry or because they need food to quell anxiety.

3

ACTIVITIES

Here are some ideas that may help you teach your child about nutrition and generally make her more comfortable in the kitchen. Remember, a child who handles food is less likely to develop food anxieties. Choose those ideas that suit your lifestyle, and discard those that do not.

KIDS-IN-THE-KITCHEN SAFETY TIPS
- Provide children with a sturdy stool.
- Knives should be sharp and stored out of reach when not in use.
- Do not put anything children might want or need above the stove. They could get burned while attempting to reach over the stove.
- Teach children to push pot handles inwards, and not to grab any pot handle without first checking to see if it's hot.
- Hair must be tied back, especially when working around a stove.
- Hands must be washed before food is touched.
- Oven mitts and apron should be at-the-ready.
- Running is not allowed in the kitchen.

KITCHEN GADGETS
(Age two and up)
- Buy plastic measuring cups and let your child play with them in the bathtub.
- An eggbeater is a gadget that will increase not only kitchen and food awareness, but coordination as well. Have your child stand over the sink and beat water. Add a little food coloring.
- Sit your child in her chair. Give her a tray, a cup, a few ice cubes and a pair of tongs. The game is to "catch" a cube, lift it and put it in the cup.

IMAGINING
(Age two and up)
Give your child a colorful cookbook to examine. Look at the pictures. What would the food in that picture taste like? Use words like sweet, bitter, salty, spicy.

SMELLING
(Age two and up)
Put different foods in little jars. Have your child close her eyes or hold a scarf up to her face (don't blindfold a young child—it's too scary) and tell her to sniff. Can she smell the dill pickles? Cheese? Apple? Orange? Chocolate?

TASTING
(Age two and up)
Have your child close her eyes. Dab "flavors" on her tongue. What is it? Lemon? Ketchup? Mild curry sauce? Let her dab food on your tongue.

DRESS THE PART
(Age two and up)

Take a white piece of cardboard, wrap it around your child's head and tape the ends. Presto! A chef's hat. If you can, buy your child a hat and apron.

KITCHEN ART
(Age two and up)

Mix up a small batch of flour paste (flour, water and a shake of salt). Use a Bristol board or some sort of cardboard. On a tray, spread out all sorts of different foods—macaroni, shell pasta, popcorn kernels, beans, peas, parsley, rice. Let your child create a collage. Once she has finished, talk about the names of the different foods. "Show me the beans." "Where is the rice?" "What's that?"

STICKERS
(Age two and up)

Collect the stickers that come on bananas. Many apples, melons, plums and peaches also carry stickers. Hang a piece of paper or cardboard on the fridge and encourage your child to paste the stickers on it.

DOLL FOOD
(Ages three and up)

Use paper plates or cut plate-size circles out of cardboard. Give your child some old food magazines (picked up at a garage sale for pennies) and let her create a paper dinner for her dolls. Simply cut the pictures out of the magazines and glue them onto the paper plates. Remember, dolls are people too, and should eat different things from the different food groups.

LOOKING
(Ages three and up)

Lay out several half-filled glasses of water. The glass should be clear. Give your child several little bottles of food coloring and let him change the color of the water. Combining different colors will also produce a third color. Let him dip white paper towels into the different glasses to see the colors better. (Children should be told not to sample the "test.")

FEELING
(Ages three and up)

Leave a few items in the bottom of a shopping bag. Have your child reach in (no peeking) and try to guess which item is which. Have her feel the difference between an apple and a pear, a tin and a jar, and so on.

COOKING
(Ages four and up)

Follow all of the kid-in-the-kitchen safety tips. Now involve your child in the cooking. Teach chopping with a small sharp knife. (Dull knives cause more cuts than sharp ones.) Have her sit at the table. Now teach her how to cut. Stay close by. She can also help with measuring and stirring ingredients.

LABELS
(Ages four and up)

Peel labels off cans and jars and stick them in an envelope. Once you have a collection:

(1) Allow your child to go through them and pick out those products she would like to buy again. Let her take the labels to the store and play match-up.

(2) Make a menu, and instead of writing in the words for the food, let her glue in the corresponding labels.

(3) Give her a sheet of Bristol board and let her make a collage. She may group all the foods by their food group (all the breads in one corner, all the vegetables in another), or she might just want to make a pretty picture.

SPELLING
(Ages five and up)

Give your child a box of alphabet pasta and let her spell out words. Add a sheet of paper plus homemade paste (flour, water, and a pinch of salt) and she can write a letter with all the pasta.

MENU
(Ages six and up)

Write the word MENU on the top of a large piece of paper. Draw boxes or squares down the page. Break the menu down into food groups: vegetables, meat, grains, fruit and so on down the page. Let your child write in the complete menu. She may read it out loud to the rest of the family just before dinner is served.

SHOPPING
(Ages six and up)

If you do allow some junk food into your home, give your child the "junk food budget." Explain to your child that munchies are fine, but most of the money must be spent on food that's high in nutritional value. However, there is $5.00 (or whatever) available for munchie food. Narrow the field to what is acceptable in your own "junk-food category." (There are some things I just can't bear to have in my house—no-name cheesies, for example.) Arguments about how many bags of chips to buy should be limited (don't ever expect them to go away). Your child will begin to make the connection between empty-calorie food and nutritional food. DO point out that veggies and dip can be the best munchie food around, AND there's no budget restriction!

•••

"I give my boys two dollars each every Friday to buy chips and pop for their home-video night. One Friday night my six-year-old said, 'If I don't want to buy anything, can I keep the money?' I said sure— why not? He saved his money and that night sat down with a plate full of raw vegetables and yogurt-based dip. He munched all the way through the movie. The next day he bought comic books. Well, his older brother saw this and decided to do like-wise. Every week I give them their treat money and every week they make their own decisions. Occa-sionally they decide to buy chips, but not often."

•••

4

TABLE MANNERS

Table Etiquette For Babies

It's in the nature of the baby to sniff and pick at her food. Accept it. It's also in the nature of the baby to don and model her cereal bowl. And it's very common for a baby/toddler to dump her cup of milk—usually over her dinner or the dog below the chair. How you handle these situations is very much part of your own past experience and your parenting style. Here are some suggestions, all of which should be taken with a cup of gentleness.

- No refills for dumped milk/juice. (There is a difference between "dumped" and "spilled." A child who accidentally spills milk should never be punished.)
- If the child removes the bib, dinner is over. Make it a sign that the meal is finished or the child is full.
- Ignore the entertainment your child puts on for your pleasure (e.g., wearing the soup bowl) and praise appropriate behavior.

- With washable felt marker or tape, mark off spots for baby's bowl and cup on her highchair tray. Help her find the right spot for each utensil.
- Reduce or eliminate your stress by placing the highchair on a few sheets of newspaper (remove the top sheet of the paper after each meal).
- A large selection of foods on a plate can be overwhelming to a child—what to eat first? Consider serving food in courses—vegetables and meats first, potatoes and more vegetables second, and so on.

The Perfect Family Dinner

Here's the scenario. Let's go super-traditional and have Mom-as-cook in this story. Apologies to dads who do the cooking.

It's Sunday night. Time for one of those Traditional Sunday Night Dinners. Out comes the creamed soup, stuffed chicken, potatoes, veggies, salad, pie, fruit and cheese tray. (Eat your heart out, June Cleaver.)

Here's a riveting dinner conversation.

"Boys, wash your hands. Dinner's ready." (Said in a mommy-voice.)

"Your hands aren't washed. Try again. Both of you—go!"

"Sit properly. Put your feet on the floor. Stop that pounding. Watch it, you'll spill…. No, it's OK, Daddy will help you clean it up. Where *is* your father? DADDY!"

"Don't throw your food. Get that bowl off your head. Don't eat until your dad and I have sat down. You said you were hungry. Eat."

"I don't want to hear you chew your food. How many times have I told you … chew with your mouth closed."

Twenty minutes later everyone is ticked off. Mom is angry because once again she has spent the better part of her Saturday or Sunday cooking, only to have the children grumble, complain and pout. And what is Daddy doing? He's tucking into dinner with gusto. He's enjoying his dinner! How dare he!

Now it doesn't take a wizard to figure out who, in this story, owns this particular problem. Mom does. Carefully and meticulously, once a week, Mom sets the scene for failure.

••

"I have this fantasy in my head of the perfect family dinner. My children all talk (happily) about their day. They eat what's put in front of them. They use their napkins. We talk about politics and events.

"Want to hear reality? My fourteen-year-old does not want to participate in this 'middle-class activity' of sitting down at the table. My twelve-year-old wants to eat in front of the TV. My eight-year-old demands mustard on everything and my three-year-old thinks that a spoon is a weapon. I give up."

••

Many parents play the fantasy of The Perfect Family Dinner over and over in their heads. It seems to be a rather harmless fantasy. What's so wrong with wanting to have a civilized meal with our kids? Is it too much to ask?

Probably.

All parents want their children to have good table manners. The way many of us go about teaching our children manners is to point out to them, and anyone within a ten mile radius, exactly what it is they're doing wrong. "Get your chin out of your soup." "Stop looking at your food and start eating it." "You're not leaving this table until you have eaten every last bite, young lady."

We are then surprised to discover that (a) children become picky eaters and (b) their manners never seem to improve.

••

"This kid could not sit on a chair. And the concept of 'elbows off the table' meant nothing. Let's not even talk about her posture. Meals were a nightmare. Last night I tossed a blanket on the floor and announced that it was 'Mexican Picnic Night'. We had a wonderful time. And she didn't put her elbows on the table once!"

••

Manners and Etiquette

Let's look at how we *can* improve our children's table manners without further alienating them from the table itself and actually turning a "trying" child into a picky eater.

Begin by explaining the meaning behind the etiquette of eating. For example, to get the last dregs of soup out of the bowl we don't tip the bowl towards us. We tip it towards the middle of the table. Why? If we slip, the soup will not pour all over us and burn us. Once explained, the chances are that now your child will tip the bowl properly.

If you don't know the explanation of how a specific ritual was developed, make one up! Tell your child not to slice open a roll and butter the whole thing. The correct way is to take the roll, break off a piece and butter that piece only. Now pop it into your mouth and chew (hopefully with the mouth closed—but don't count on it). Why should you not coat the whole roll in butter? Ahhhhhhhhhh—because you might not finish the roll and ahhhhhhhhhh—we can't feed buttered rolls to birds because—ahhhhhhhhhh—we don't want birds to develop high cholesterol. (OK, a silly example, but the idea is to have a little fun. Children know when we are stretching the truth.)

Enter the silverware. To some adults the tableware for a four-course meal is intimidating. It's no less so to small children. Set your own table in the traditional pattern, working from the outside in. Confused?

If the first course is salad, lay the salad fork to the left on the outside. Lay the salad knife on the outside to the right. In other words, working from the outside in. As each course comes, all you do is pick up the next utensil. Naturally others will set the table differently. That doesn't matter. Soon your child will begin to match the shape of the utensil with the meal; e.g., the soupspoon is big, the bread knife is little and cute, the steak knife is sharp, the fish fork is funny-looking and so on.

Let your child set the table. Buy plain placemats and with a permanent felt marker outline the place setting. All he has to do is place each piece of cutlery on the drawing.

Better yet, tell your child the menu and let him guess what utensils are needed.

Use candles at least once a week and/or dim the lights. As a rule, the lower the lights, the quieter the conversation. Besides, it's fun.

Treat your children like guests and chances are they will behave like guests. (They still have to do their share of the clean-up, however.)

••

"My children behave infinitely better around the dining-room table than they do around the kitchen table."
••

Try not to correct your child at the table. Mention inappropriate behavior later, but *only* if you can point out several things your child did right. Example: "Chris, you sat on your chair through-out the entire meal. I'm proud of you. I bet next time you'll remember to use your napkin, too." Children don't need to be hit over the head with explanations—they'll get the point.

Where do children learn table etiquette? From us. Dad belches at the table, laughs about it and says (yet again), "Gee, in some countries a good belch after a meal is a compliment, ha ha ha." The children are listening. In some cases a boy (especially) will notice his mom's disapproving reaction to daddy's belch and think that good manners are sissy stuff.

Parents who toss the utensils in the middle of the table and expect the children to grab what they need are showing children that etiquette is not important, or that it's reserved for company only.

Then there is the Curse of the TV tray. No need to chew with their mouths closed if their dinner partner is the boob tube. Our lives are busy, chaotic even, but children will never learn any table manners wolfing down a meal while watching TV or perched at the kitchen counter.

Good table manners are an extension of good manners. They are needed everyday and must be practised by all.

OK, death-by-poor-manners is not likely, but people with poor table etiquette have been known not to make the deal, climb the ladder or get invited back. Besides, no one can enjoy a meal if he is uncomfortable, and both children and adults will be uncomfortable at a table if they think they are making idiots of themselves. That having been said, it's still better to have peace at the table and have children enjoy being together as a family than to have perfect manners. Time is on your side.

If all else fails, wait until your child is a teenager and then take him and his girlfriend out to a snazzy restaurant. You may be surprised to discover that he has known all along how to behave and how to act. Or, if he hasn't learned a darn thing, you can be sure that he'll clean up his act p.d.q. just to impress his girlfriend. (You're in trouble if your child's date has worse table manners than your child.)

Is it wrong to fantasize about The Perfect Family Meal? Absolutely not. But make it a goal to strive for. Think of each meal as a tiny step towards that goal and shrug off those tiny steps back.

A final word about manners. One day your children will have their own children. Suddenly their manners will be impeccable. It's a fact.

Serve It Up

Presentation may not be everything but it's a big part of appeasing the picky eater. Add a little humor, a lot of love and picky-eater tendencies may not disappear but they will be lessened.

- Some children do not like their foods to "touch." If the peas nudge the potatoes, both vegetables are now uneatable. Avoid the inevitable argument and serve the meal in a TV-dinner-type tray. (One clever mom divided up her son's plate with long, thin, raw carrot strips. Her son's demand lasted two weeks.)
- Many cooks make up individual plates at the stove and plunk them down in front of each person. Without words, the child has been told what to eat and how much. Try putting the food on serving dishes and let family members help themselves.

••

"I usually make four dishes per meal. Each child may pass up *one* dish only."

••

••

"We encourage our children to be very trying— and believe me, they are. Each child must *try* everything being offered. One bite is enough. No more is said."

••

- Banana Leaf restaurants are very popular in Singapore. Dinner is served up on huge banana leaves. Neat. All right, banana leaves might not be all that common in our neighborhoods, but who says that all food must be served on a plate? Serve up a special hamburger dinner on a frisbee or fish sticks in a plastic boat. Heaven knows what you can put in little wicker or plastic baskets!

- Chopsticks, anyone? Learning how to wield chopsticks is now *de rigueur*. Might as well start the kids off early. Chinese chopsticks are long and thick with blunt ends. Japanese chopsticks are smaller, thin and have pointy ends. I prefer Japanese-style chopsticks while my kids prefer Chinese. Upshot, it's an individual preference. Very cheap, disposable wooden chopsticks may give splinters. Opt for the mid-priced, non-disposable types.

Now, take a pair of chopsticks and fold a piece of cardboard (match-cover size) in half. Put the folded cardboard at the handle end of the two chopsticks. Wind an elastic band around the chopsticks and the cardboard. The chopsticks will now act like giant tweezers. Place them in your child's hand, reminding her to try to keep the bottom stick stable while moving only the top stick. Piercing food is just not done.

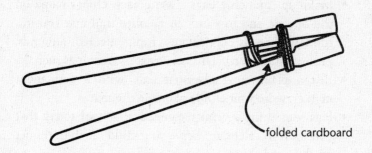

folded cardboard

- Young children often find that Chinese soupspoons are easier to manage than most other spoons.
- Toss a blanket under the table and pitch a sheet over the top. Now crawl under and have lunch in a tent.
- It's hard to be the youngest. Big brother and sister take a lunch to school. Pack your toddler's lunch in his own lunchbox and have lunch in the playroom or park, or at the kitchen table for that matter.

••

"I sometimes combine two different types of canned soup—perhaps minestrone and chicken noodle, or mushroom and oyster. Last night I put vegetable and tomato soup together. My five-year-old loved it and asked what kind of soup it was. I told her that I had mixed two different cans of soup together. She gasped and said, 'Are you *allowed* to do that?'"

••

- Taste-testing is a fine idea, but beware; if your four children taste-test four different types of ketchup, they will like and demand that you keep four different types of ketchup on hand. *Now* if you choose one ketchup, you'll end up with, "You chose that one 'cause you like Amanda best!"
- Make up "munchie bags." Write each child's name on the outside and toss in your favorite trail mix (raisins, sunflower seeds, chocolate chips, slivered almonds, peanuts and so on). This is a "treat"—treat it as such.
- Buy a plain vinyl placemat and, with a permanent marker, write your child's name on the mat.
- Has something special happened at school today that you want to celebrate? Serve your child lunch or dinner on the good china.

A word about the good China—a plate is a plate—it's replace-able. A child is not replaceable. If your china is so valuable that you know that you would become terribly upset if a piece were broken, pack it away until the children are older. To quote a little friend, "You can get a new dish but you can't get a new me."

5

THE TWO-CAREER FAMILY

The Guilt Factor

Mom and Dad get up at 6:00. They shower, dress, gulp down a coffee, make lunches. At 6:45 it's time to get the kids up. Bedlam. Dress 'em, feed 'em, hug 'em, pop one out the door to catch a bus and lug one over to daycare. Mom and Dad catch the 8:15 train and land at work at 9:00. Whew!

The end of the day routine is no easier, except that now Mom and Dad are tired. Child and baby are picked up. Everyone tumbles into the house with briefcases, diaper bags, schoolbags and shopping bags. Now, does Mom or Dad feel like preparing a big meal? Does anyone feel like sitting down at a table and carrying on an animated conversation? Does anyone feel like eating? (Oops! Don't forget it's Brownie night. Gotta' leave at 7:00.)

The connection between guilt and meal preparation is an interesting one. On top of that, many parents *still* feel that unless they put a substantial amount of time into preparing dinner, they have failed their family somehow. For example, years ago a new and improved cake mix was released. All one had to do with the mix was add water and bake. It was as good as any other mix on the market, and easier to use. But it bombed in the marketplace. Why? It was discovered that moms baked cakes to show their families that they cared. Mixing water into a mix was just not enough effort. Many working mothers feel the same way—they feel that unless they put effort into the meal preparation they are not living up to their own expectations.

> "I have to work—no, I *want* to work. I don't know why I am defending myself. But I still want my children to have a normal family life, and to me that means that they should have healthy, balanced meals around the table. But I'm so tired when I get home. The kids are always famished, everyone wants to eat immediately—I can't tell you how often we end up with take-out or snacks."

How does this relate to the picky eater?

Let's say that Mom, despite a hectic schedule, does invest a substantial amount of time in the food preparation. Perhaps the weekend is reserved for making up batches of meals. How is Mom going to react to the child who says, "Yuck, I don't like it"? Chances are Mom overreacts, and hollers, "JUST EAT IT." Child yells back "NO." And a battle that a parent cannot win, begins. The child may now relate food to fights.

Tips for the Two-Income Family:

GOOD MORNING

- Breakfast is often the first victim of the hurry-up generation. Check out the breakfast section in this book. Remember, it's better to eat a big meal in the morning than at night. Leftovers such as spaghetti, meat loaf, pizza and so on are good for children and take only seconds to heat in a microwave.

- Oops, you've overslept. Put dry cereal in a bag and let your child munch as you drive to the babysitter's. (Let Fido give the back seat a once-over to clean up. Who said these tips must pass Miss Manners' inspection?)

- Keep breakfast bars on hand. Homemade ones are great, but in a fix, most commercial bars will do.

- Toss an egg, milk and two drops of vanilla in the blender. Whirl. Bottle it and let Toddler-Sue drink her eggnog as you drive.

HOME AGAIN

- Walk in the door and immediately present an appetizer. Consider it part of dinner. Raw vegetables and dip are great, but must be prepared in advance. Cheese and bread are fine as long as they are used to allay appetite and not appease it altogether. A cut-up tofu dog skewered with a straight pretzel, with mustard as a dip, may buy you some time. (Tofu dogs can be found at your local health-food store. Don't tell the family what they are made of. Just serve them and see what happens.)

- Children who are involved in the process of preparing food are more likely to eat that food. Give everyone a mealtime job. Even three-year-olds can wash lettuce.

- Teach your children to make a few simple meals themselves. Small children can, for example, make a salad bar for the whole family.
- Keep chopped, frozen vegetables in your freezer. Add them to just about everything.
- Some children like to munch on frozen peas as a snack. Well, why not?
- Divide up the meal. Serve an appetizer as soon as you get home, dinner one hour later.
- Give your child a tiny serving of what's to come—a few teaspoons of stew, for example. Ward off hunger—don't destroy it.
- Equip your family for your lifestyle, not your parents' lifestyle. Buy a microwave, a crock pot and a dishwasher (sell the sofa if you have to). For the family that has one parent at home, these items might be considered luxuries. For a two-income family, they are necessities. (Now learn to use the microwave for more than defrosting chicken and reheating coffee.)
- Make extra helpings of favorite foods and freeze them in individual-size servings for a "freezer-meal night."

Here's a speedy appetizer with kid-appeal.

Peel a pink grapefruit and cut it into sections. Using four or five plates, make individual servings. Make a bed of lettuce on each plate. Spread the grapefruit on the bed of lettuce. Open a can of crab meat, plop it on top of grapefruit. Top with a sauce of equal parts ketchup and mayonnaise. Serve.

Look at the food groups that you have just covered!

There are any number of presto recipes you can use. The point is: buy yourself some time. Now sit down and have a cup of tea and ask your children about their day.

WARNING! Most accidents, including accidental child poisonings, take place before dinner, typically between 5:00 and 6:00 p.m. This time has been dubbed "the arsenic hour." The reason is that everyone is tired and preoccupied, and children are thirsty or hungry and more inclined to "snack" on a few pills. All pills are potentially harmful to children, but iron and vitamin pills are particularly dangerous because many adults do not perceive them as poisonous and leave them out in the open.

About Fast Foods

"I once asked my Grade 2 class to tell me what number they would dial in an emergency. At least half of them gave me the phone number of a popular pizza parlor."

"Get in the car, we're going for burgers." Now *there's* a cry with a familiar ring.

Even the pickiest of picky eaters will eat something in a fast-food restaurant (although I have known one little fellow to return from a sixty-item salad bar with one lettuce leaf on his plate). Should a parent take a child into a fast-food restaurant? Doesn't this set a precedent? After all, the scary nutritional wisdom says that this food will lie in wait in our arteries until the time comes when, with murder in mind, it will clog them up and kill us.

There is absolutely no doubt that a high-fat diet is something to be avoided. However, before fast-food restaurants are banned altogether, think about the big picture.

....

"If you had asked me last month how often I took my eight-year-old to a fast-food restaurant I would probably have told you a couple of times a month. Then I added it up. Twice a week we go swimming with a friend and her child, and then out for a snack. We usually end up eating out on Saturday— our errand day. I teach an evening course, so I often order in once a week. And it's not uncommon for my husband to bring home take-out every once in a while. Counting it up, we eat fast food at least five times a week!"

....

Fast-food restaurants play a role in our lives and in our children's social life. This role can start very early in life if there is a restaurant nearby or on the way home from school. Should this be of concern? Yes and no.

One study of the eating habits of young girls discovered that young girls do make sensible food choices as a rule.

Children use fast food as a way to bond with other kids. If fast food is banned on the home front, children may use fast food to rebel. (Given the types of rebellion available, most parents would see french-fry consumption as fairly harmless, especially if the children are eating well otherwise and are of normal weight.)

Banning fast food altogether or not allowing a child to visit a fast-food restaurant with her friends may alienate the child from her peer group. Chances are a child will break the rules and go anyway, and end up secretive and guilty.

Most of us accept that these restaurants are part of our lives. The goal now is to start making better choices at the order desk. Salad bars are great, assuming one doesn't smear half a cup of blue-cheese dressing on top of the salad. And hold the special sauce—dress your own burgers. Naturally, one always orders milk instead of pop—naturally. The point is, we can *show* our children how to eat at a fast-food restaurant.

We can also explain to children why it is we do not want them to eat too much fast food. (It's amazing how many parents will simply use "don't" as an explanation.)

We don't want our children to turn into number-crunching calorie counters. Children should be taught to see the total picture of their food intake. That being so, a child should still have an idea that certain foods can really add on the weight while only providing minimal nutritional value.

....

"I overheard my friend say to her seven-year-old, 'You're getting too chubby, stop eating so much.' The look on his face was one of total confusion. He turned and said, 'What's food got to do with getting fat?'"

....

Tips
- "You did great, kid. Let's celebrate. How about going to Hamburger Delicious for dinner?" Regularly using food as a reward is not a good idea. Try this instead, "You did great, kid. Let's celebrate. How about we take in a movie or go to the zoo?"
- Instead of throwing your child's birthday party in a fast-food restaurant, opt for the museum, a science center, or the park—a party need not revolve around food.
- Eat before going to a movie. If you must buy treats at the snack bar, get unbuttered or "untopped" popcorn.
- Most of us order-in food more times than we'd care to admit. It's a good idea to find a few delivery-type restaurants which will, if asked, take special requests, e.g., to hold the MSG, or to list the ingredients (if there is an allergy in the house).

• •

"My children can eat a box of cookies in one sitting. As if that wasn't annoying enough, they then take the empty box and put it back in the cupboard. Mind you, that's the only time a cookie-box stays in the cupboard for longer than three days."

• •

Food Allergies

An allergic food reaction may occur when a child has a bad response after eating a specific food.

Children suffering an allergic food reaction soon after the food is eaten may vomit, experience nausea, stomach pain or diarrhea. Their lips and face may become swollen. They may have breathing problems, become congested, cough or collapse and fall into shock. Sometimes just smelling the food can bring on a reaction.

Foods which typically seem to cause these kinds of reactions are: peanuts, nuts, fish, shellfish and eggs.

If your child displays any sort of swelling or breathing problem or collapses, RUSH your child to the nearest hospital. THIS IS A MEDICAL EMERGENCY.

Reactions to foods may sometimes be less violent. Children suffering milder reactions may experience abdominal pain, nausea, diarrhea, constipation, eczema, chronic hives, insomnia, bad breath, hyperactivity, wheezing, coughing or nasal congestion. These symptoms may occur many hours after eating the food.

Foods which typically seem to cause these kinds of reactions are: milk, wheat, eggs, corn and soy.

Children with an eating problem should be investigated for food allergies or other medically based eating problems such as celiac disease or diabetes.

6

OUR DAILY MEALS, PLUS SNACKS

Breakfast

The trick of getting the children to eat a great breakfast is (1) to get up early and (2) to get rid of the idea that a good breakfast consists of two or three specific foods. Where is it written that we must eat cereal or eggs in the morning? Let's expand our horizons here. What we're looking for in a good breakfast is speed (it must take less than five minutes to prepare), nutrition and enjoyment.

••

"I grew up eating sole, spaghetti, kippers and leftovers for breakfast. The first time I slept over at a friend's house and saw what she ate—cereal floating around in a bowl of milk, greasy sausages and bacon—I was nearly ill."

••

- White fish such as fillet of sole can be battered the night before. In the morning fry it up in a nonstick pan.

- Microwave corn on the cob. Remove most of the outer husk. Microwave on high for 5 minutes, turning once. Let sit for 2 more minutes. If it's still too crunchy, zap it again. Do not let children remove the husks. They may be too hot.
- When making spaghetti for dinner, cook double the amount needed. (Easy to do since blessed few of us can ever cook the right amount of noodles.) Using several individual microwave dishes, put one serving in each and top with sauce. Freeze. To defrost in the morning, pop spaghetti into the microwave on defrost (30%) for 5 to 8 minutes. (Take a shower.) Mike it on reheat for 2 minutes longer. (Find Christie's hair clips, Will's basketball shirt, remind Robbie to leave a little toothpaste in the tube.) Spaghetti is now ready. Serve with milk to drink.
- When making pancakes on a Sunday morning, triple the batch. Freeze pancakes in individual plastic bags. Defrost during the week in the microwave. Depending on their size they may also be defrosted in the toaster. (You may have to run the pancake through the toaster twice.)
- Syrup on pancakes may be the Canadian thing to do, but honey is also tasty. Buy or put honey in a mustard-type squeeze-bottle for less mess. Or spread jam on pancakes.
- Make a banana kabob. Cut up a firm banana into bite-size chunks. Wrap a slice of bacon around each chunk. Thread chunks on to skewers. Broil for 2 to 3 minutes. Turn. Broil for 2 minutes longer. (Great over an open fire when camping.)
- When passing the frozen food section, think breakfast not dinner. If Robbie likes lamb chops, why can't he have them for breakfast?

....

"We had a Christmas tree decorated with Cheerios strung on string one year. It was interesting—to say the least."
....

- Breakfast is an excellent time to eat beans. Serve beans on toast. (Beans are high-fiber food and will cause bum-burps. Once the system is used to the fiber, this little problem will, er, pass.)

- Leftover rice quickly stir-fried with vegetables is wonderful in the morning. Keep a bag of frozen, chopped vegetables in the freezer. Run a handful of frozen veggies under water for a few seconds and then toss them in a wok or pan with a tablespoon of oil. Stir. Add last night's rice. Stir.

- On a day when you have the time, make a face on the plate. Take one fried egg sunny side up. Make a smile on the egg with a slice of cheese. Add two raisins for eyes. A little chunk of cheese run through a garlic crusher can be the hair.

- Make a "Sun-in-the-window." Fry an egg, toast a piece of bread. Use a cookie-cutter to cut out a circle. Place the toast over the egg so it peeks out.

- Boil an egg. The yolk should be runny. Cut toast into five long "fingers" for dipping.

- Make a basket for scrambled eggs. Flatten bread with a rolling pin. Butter one side of the bread. Spray a muffin pan with nonstick spray (or oil a tray if preferred). Press the bread into the tin, butter side up. Bake at 400°F (200°C) for 5 minutes. Make scrambled eggs. Put eggs in the "nest" and serve.

- Cheese Dreams are a favorite. Toast a piece of bread. Cover the toast with a slice of Cheddar cheese and pop under the broiler for 1 minute.

••

"I loved boiled eggs because of a little game I used to play with my granny. I'd gobble down the egg as fast as I could and then turn the shell over and say, 'Look, I haven't eaten my egg and I'm not going to.' My granny would scold me and carry on until I said, 'Surprise, my egg's all gone.' I still love boiled eggs."

••

- Cereals sometimes taste best without milk. And when it comes to bed-time snacks, a bowl of cereal for a night-time "breakfast" tastes wonderful. In fact, cold cereals can pop up almost any time of the day.
- Put cereal in a wide cup instead of a bowl. Children can then drink up the last of the milk.
- Add some trail mix to a bowl of cereal for a snack. Serve with or without milk.
- On St. Patrick's Day, add a drop of green food coloring to oatmeal. On Valentine's Day, add red food coloring.
- Put strawberries in a bowl, along with grapes, sliced apples and whatever other fruit is on hand. Mix a teaspoon of honey with an individual-size container of plain yogurt. Pour over fruit. Divide into bowls.

BANANA SPLIT BREKKY

1 banana	1
$\frac{1}{2}$ cup favorite yogurt	125 ml
2 tbsp granola (or favorite cereal)	30 ml

Chop banana into thick slices and place in bowl. Top with yogurt and sprinkle with cereal. A strawberry perched on top would be most attractive.

PANCAKES

1 egg	1
$\frac{3}{4}$ cup milk	175 ml
3 tbsp butter, melted	45 ml
$1\frac{1}{2}$ cup flour	375 ml
2 tbsp sugar	30 ml
$2\frac{1}{2}$ tsp baking soda	12 ml
$\frac{1}{2}$ tsp salt (or less)	2ml

Beat egg until fluffy and mix with milk and butter. Add remaining ingredients. Mix. Add more milk if too thick. Cook pancakes on greased griddle until bubbles appear in batter. Flip. Cook on other side until light brown.

MORE PANCAKES

Pineapple Pancakes. Add $\frac{1}{2}$ cup (125 ml) canned pineapple, drained and chopped, to pancake mix.

Banana Pancakes. Beat 1 chopped banana plus $\frac{1}{2}$ tsp (2 ml) nutmeg into pancake mixture.

Orange Juice Pancakes. Add 2 tbsp (30 ml) concentrated orange juice plus 1 small orange (cut into tiny chunks) to pancake mixture.

Blueberry Pancakes. Mix $\frac{1}{2}$ to $\frac{1}{3}$ cup (125 to 150 ml) fresh blueberries into pancake mixture. (Frozen blueberries may be substituted. It's not necessary to thaw the berries first.)

Serve extra pancakes with tea and jam later on in the day. Teddy bears and dollies are also known to find pancake and jam sandwiches very tasty.

Instant Breakfast

Oops! No time for breakfast. Or, your child simply won't eat breakfast. Or, your child has an hour's bus ride and if she doesn't have anything to eat on the bus she'll raid her lunch. A suggestion: hand your child a bar of something as she dashes out of the door. Here are two favorite recipes.

BREKKY BARS

1 cup margarine	250 ml
$\frac{1}{2}$ cup chunky peanut butter	125 ml
1 cup packed brown sugar	250 ml
2 eggs	2
1 cup honey	250 ml
2 cups whole-wheat flour	500 ml
2 cups oatmeal	500 ml
1 cup wheat germ	250 ml
$\frac{1}{2}$ tsp vanilla	2ml
1 cup raisins	250 ml
1 cup chopped salted peanuts (or ground almonds)	250 ml

Beat margarine, peanut butter and brown sugar until creamy. Add eggs, one at a time, and then honey. Beat until fluffy. In a separate bowl mix flour, oats and wheat germ, and add to the peanut butter mixture. Add vanilla to raisins. Mix vanilla-soaked raisins into peanut mixture and combine with flour mixture. Drop by the teaspoon on cookie sheet. Bake at 375°F (190°C) for 10 to 12 minutes.

JENNIFER'S BARS (JENNIFER WEBBER)

$\frac{1}{2}$ cup margarine	125 ml
$\frac{1}{2}$ lb pack marshmallows	250 g
5 cups cornflakes or honey-nut cornflakes	1.25 L
1 cup chopped dates and apricots	250 ml
1 cup sliced almonds	250 ml
$\frac{1}{2}$ cup unsalted sunflower seeds	125 ml
$\frac{1}{2}$ cup sesame seeds	50 ml

Melt margarine and marshmallows. (Can be done in the microwave.) Stir in remaining ingredients. Press into greased, oblong pan (9" x 11"/23 x 28 cm). Cut into squares when cool.

PURPLE OATMEAL

Follow the package instructions to make 1 serving of oatmeal. Before cooking add:

$\frac{1}{2}$ cup raisins	125 ml
2 tbsp grape jelly	30 ml

Cook or microwave according to instructions.

FRUIT OATMEAL

Follow the package instructions to make 1 serving of oatmeal. Before cooking add:

$\frac{1}{4}$ cup sliced banana	50 ml
$\frac{1}{4}$ cup berries	50 ml
2 tbsp raisins	30 ml

1 tbsp brown sugar	15 ml
$\frac{1}{4}$ tsp cinnamon	1 ml

Cook according to instructions. Sprinkle with chopped fruit or nuts.

SMOOTHIES
(To be made in the blender or food processor.)
A word about raw eggs. The risk of poisoning from raw eggs in Canada is small, but caution is still needed. Choose clean, uncracked eggs. Keep them refrigerated. Do not make an eggnog (for example) ahead of time. Once the egg is broken, mix and serve right away. Do not serve a raw egg in any form to a baby under one year.

THE CLASSIC

1 egg	1
1 cup milk	250 ml
1 banana	1
2 drops of vanilla extract	2 drops

Whirl. (Add 1 tsp (5 ml) of honey if you like.)

CHOCOLATE SHAKE CLASSIC

1 egg	1
1 tbsp powdered hot chocolate mix	15 ml
1 cup milk	250 ml

Whirl.

TERRIFIC TYLER (JAYNE STAFFORD)

1 frozen banana	1
1 cup frozen strawberries	250 ml
2 cups apple juice	500 ml

Blend until smooth. Add more juice to thin if desired.

BANANA AND STRAWBERRY WHIP

1 banana	1
1 cup strawberries (frozen or fresh)	250 ml
1 cup milk	250 ml
1 tsp honey	5 ml

Whirl.

• •

Pour leftover juice smoothies into ice-cube trays. Pop them out and use as cooling floats in drinks.

• •

BANANA SMOOTHIE

1 cup milk	250 ml
1 medium banana	1
1 tbsp honey	15 ml
$\frac{1}{2}$ tsp vanilla	2 ml

Whirl.

BEST BANANA

$\frac{1}{2}$ cup milk	125 ml
$\frac{1}{2}$ banana	$\frac{1}{2}$

$\frac{1}{2}$ tsp vanilla	2 ml
shake of cinnamon	

Whirl with ice cube.

Choco-Banana

1 cup chocolate frozen yogurt	250 ml
1 ripe banana	1
1 egg	1
1 tbsp wheat germ	15 ml
1 to 1$\frac{1}{2}$ cup milk	250 to 375 ml

Whirl.

Strawberry Smoothie

$\frac{1}{2}$ cup milk	125 ml
$\frac{1}{2}$ cup vanilla yogurt	125 ml
$\frac{1}{2}$ cup frozen strawberries	125 ml
1 tsp sugar	5 ml

Whirl.

Frozen Berry

$\frac{1}{2}$ cup frozen strawberries or raspberries	125 ml
$\frac{1}{2}$ cup plain yogurt	125 ml
$\frac{1}{4}$ tsp vanilla	1 ml
1 tsp honey	5 ml

Whirl.

Note: Add a little milk to thin if neccessary.

BETTER BUTTER BANANA

1 cup milk	250 ml
1 frozen banana	1
2 tbsp peanut butter	30 ml
drop of vanilla	1 drop

Whirl.

ORANGE WHIRL

$\frac{1}{2}$ cup milk	125 ml
$\frac{1}{2}$ cup fresh orange juice	125 ml

Whirl.

ORANGE TOSS

1 cup orange juice	250 ml
$\frac{1}{2}$ cup frozen vanilla yogurt	125 ml

Whirl.

APRICOT SMOOTHIE

$\frac{1}{2}$ lb dried apricots	250 g
$\frac{1}{2}$ cup milk	125 ml

Soak in water (to cover) for 1 to 2 hours or until soft. Drain, reserving 2 to 4 tsp (5 to 10 ml) of the water. Blend apricots with reserved water until smooth. Strain, and add milk. Whirl.

Orange Yogurt Whip

$\frac{1}{2}$ cup plain yogurt	125 ml
$\frac{1}{2}$ cup orange juice	125 ml
1 tbsp honey	15 ml

Whirl.

••

Tip: For a really speedy drink for a toddler, pour cold milk or plain yogurt, whirled first in the blender, into an almost-empty jam jar. Shake well and pour.

••

Mighty Melon

$\frac{1}{2}$ cup honeydew or cantaloupe chunks	125 ml
$\frac{1}{2}$ cup grape juice	125 ml

Whirl with a few ice cubes.

Melon for My Honey

1 cup honeydew melon chunks	250 ml
1 peach, peeled and pitted	1
1 cup orange juice	250 ml

Whirl.

Heady Pineapple

1 cup pineapple juice	250 ml
1 cup cranberry juice	250 ml
$\frac{1}{2}$ cup tofu	125 ml

Whirl. Serve chilled.

VEGGIE WHIP

2 chopped carrots	2
1 chopped celery stick	1
$\frac{1}{2}$ tsp chopped parsley	2 ml
1 tsp Worcestershire sauce	5 ml
1 tsp lemon juice	5 ml
$\frac{1}{2}$ cup tomato juice	125 ml

Blend at high speed in food processor until smooth. Add a little water if it's too thick. Strain through sieve. Makes 2 small servings.

Lunchtime

••

"My son's lunchbox contained raw carrots, a sandwich on brown bread, one apple, an orange and a cookie from the health-food store. He never ate it, of course. If I were to be entirely honest about it, I'd say that I made his lunch for show. The lunchroom monitors were volunteer moms."

••

Lunchbox rules

(1) Follow the lunchbox code. If applesauce is considered by your child or his peers as "baby food," don't send it.
(2) Get your child involved in preparing his or her own lunch.
(3) Don't ever, not ever, tuck a mushy note in your child's lunchbox. If that note falls into the wrong hands, your child won't forgive you until he has children of his own—if then.
(4) Decorate your child's lunchbag with cute drawings if he or she is in kindergarten. After that, forget it.

The Picky Eater

(5) Don't display your child's name on her lunchbox for all to read. Write her name on the inside of the box. Decorate the outside of your child's box with stickers or a felt-marker design—anything that makes it identifiable amongst all the other lunchboxes in the school. Let your child decide what the decoration should be.

Tuck jokes into your child's lunchbox. Buy a silly joke book and keep it hidden in a kitchen drawer. Here are a few jokes to tide you over until you get to the bookstore:

What's round and red and goes up and down?
A tomato in an elevator.

What room has no doors?
A mushroom.

How many sides does a square box have?
Two. The inside and the outside.

What classroom table doesn't have any legs?
The multiplication table.

Who can tell the class when the Iron Age ended?
When drip-dry clothes were invented.

What insect does well in school?
The spelling bee.

PITA-PIZZA ROLLS

16- or 19-oz can crushed pineapple	500 ml or 540 ml can
1 small package cream cheese	1
$\frac{1}{3}$ cup mayonnaise (or less)	75 ml
1 tbsp tomato paste	15 ml
$\frac{1}{2}$ lb ham	250 g
1 cup Mozzarella cheese	250 ml
1 small green pepper	1

Combine drained pineapple chunks with cream cheese, mayonnaise and tomato paste. Open pita pocket. Put in mixture. Cut ham into cubes. Grate Mozzarella cheese. Cut green pepper into strips. Top mixture with ham chunks, Mozzarella cheese and green pepper strips.

Children love this cold in a lunch bag. Or, wrap in foil and heat at 350°F (180°C) for 15 minutes or until cheese is melted and bubbly.

BRUSCHETTA

(Call this one a pizza stick.)

French stick (baguette)	1
1 tbsp olive oil	15 ml
1 clove garlic, minced	1
1 tbsp dried basil	15 ml
1 tbsp dried oregano	15 ml
6 tbsp grated Parmesan cheese	90 ml

Cut stick in half lengthwise and toast under broiler for 2 minutes (or less). Mix spices with oil and spread on toasted stick. Dust with cheese. Heat under broiler for 2 minutes. Serve warm.

Note: Add 1 tbsp (15 ml) of spaghetti sauce and 1 thinly sliced tomato plus the remaining ingredients for that "pizza parlor" touch. And by all means let the children create their own pizza sticks. But remember, toast the stick first or the ingredients will sink into the bread and make a mushy mess.

FRUITY PEANUT BUTTER

2 tbsp peanut butter	30 ml
1 tbsp raisins	15 ml
2 slices bread	2

Mix peanut butter and raisins together and spread on bread.

Alternative: Mix $1/2$ cup (125 ml) of peanut butter with a handful of trail mix. (Chop any large pieces of dried fruit or nuts.) Keep this peanut-butter/trail-mix mixture in a jar in the fridge and use as you would any sandwich spread.

CURRY IN A BAGEL

2 tsp curry powder	10 ml
$\frac{1}{4}$ tsp turmeric	1 ml
2 cups cooked chicken	500 ml
1 apple*	1
1 tsp lemon juice	5 ml
$\frac{1}{2}$ cup cream cheese	125 ml
4 bagels	4

Heat curry powder and turmeric in dry pan for 2 minutes, stirring constantly. Cool. Chop chicken. Peel, core and chop apple. Toss apple with lemon juice. Combine spices with remaining ingredients. Spread on bagels. Wrap.

*Alternative: Substitute stick of celery for apple.

Note: These can be frozen at the beginning of the week. Take them out of the freezer in the morning. In warm weather the sandwich will be defrosted, but still cool, by lunchtime.

••

"I got a call from my six-year-old's teacher. She wondered if my daughter was not eating enough lunch. Odd, I thought. I packed her quite a big lunch. I told the teacher that I'd make it a little bigger. Two weeks later I got a call from the principal. She wanted to know if there were any problems at home. Curious and more curious. I took a day off work, drove my daughter to school and sat in the back of the classroom. I didn't see any problems. Finally another mother called and asked me point blank, why was it that I sent my daughter to school with only an apple for lunch! I finally discovered that my daughter, who took an hour's bus ride to school every morning, was, out of sheer boredom, eating her entire lunch before arriving at school."

••

ZUCCHINI ROLLS

1 medium-size zucchini	1
$\frac{1}{2}$ cup Cheddar cheese	125 ml
$\frac{1}{4}$ cup cottage cheese	50 ml

Cut top and bottom off of zucchini. Cut zucchini into 3-inch (8 cm) chunks and hollow out. Place on paper towel to dry out. Store in fridge for 1 hour. Blend Cheddar and cottage cheese together in food processor. Spoon into zucchini and chill. Cut into thin slices to make zucchini wheels.

Alternative: Add carrot shavings, 1 tsp (5 ml) hot mustard and a little fresh parsley to mixture for a more adult taste.

Note: Zucchini come in all sizes. This recipe works well with a 9-inch (23 cm) zucchini, but use your own judgment.

Tofu Egg Salad

$\frac{1}{2}$ cake tofu	$\frac{1}{2}$
1 hard-boiled egg	1
1 celery stalk, chopped	1
2 tbsp mayonnaise	30 ml
pepper to taste	

Combine tofu and egg. Mash, and add chopped celery and mayonnaise. Fill pita bread with mixture.

Note: If your children do not like hard-boiled eggs, try omitting the egg altogether. If the taste is not zesty enough, add a tablespoon (15 ml) of tamari sauce to one tablespoon (15 ml) of mayonnaise. Mix with tofu.

Flat Fried Cheese

1 slice Canadian Cheddar
2 slices favorite bread
margarine
2 gherkin pickles

Make a cheese sandwich. Cut gherkins into strips and place on cheese. Spread margarine on outside of sandwich, and fry in frying pan. Squash down flat.

CREAM CHEESE AND TRAIL MIX

2 tbsp cream cheese	30 ml
2 tbsp trail mix (sunflower seeds, raisins, mixed nuts, etc.)	30 ml
2 slices tomato	2
shredded lettuce	

Mix cream cheese with trail mix. Fill pita pocket, and top with tomato slices and shredded lettuce.

CREAM CHEESE AND PINEAPPLE DOTS

2 tbsp cream cheese	30 ml
2 tbsp chopped pineapple	30 ml

Mix and spread on bread.

BAKED POTATO TO GO

1 baked potato	1
1 tbsp Cheddar cheese	15 ml
2 tbsp cubed ham	30 ml
2 tbsp plain yogurt	30 ml

Cut potato in half and scoop out insides (potato can be warm or cold). Mash most of pulp with all remaining ingredients. Stuff back into potato. Wrap tightly.

WEENIES AND BEANS

4 jumbo hot dogs	4
prepared mustard	
14-oz can beans	398 ml

4 strips bacon	4
4 jumbo hot dog rolls	4

Split hot dogs lengthwise, but don't go through the meat all the way. Coat inside of hot dog with mustard. Scoop in 2 tbsp (30 ml) of beans per dog. Wrap each dog with strip of bacon. Secure with skewer. Grill until the bacon is cooked. Serve on toasted buns with extra beans on the side.

Alternative: Substitute Cheddar cheese for beans.

I-LOVE-YOU CREAM CHEESE

2 tbsp cream cheese	30 ml
2 drops red food coloring	2
2 drops milk	2

Mix and spread on bread. Serve open-face. Or cut bread into the shape of a heart.

ELEGANT SALMON

$7\frac{1}{2}$-oz can salmon	213 g
$\frac{1}{4}$ cup light cream cheese	50 ml
1 tbsp chopped celery (optional)	15 ml
1 tbsp capers (optional)	15 ml
$\frac{1}{2}$ tsp horseradish (optional)	2 ml

Drain salmon and mash with cream cheese and remaining ingredients, if desired. Spread on bread. Makes enough filling for 6 small-to-medium sandwiches.

Note: These sandwiches can be frozen.

Lunch at Home and Away

Spread peanut butter on bread and put under the broiler for 1 to 2 minutes. Pull it out when it bubbles. Very nutty.

Add chopped gherkin pickles to 2 tbsp (30 ml) of peanut butter. Spread on bread or crackers.

Try substituting a crêpe for bread or a pita pocket. Simply spread your favorite filling on the crêpe and roll it up.

Just about anything can be stuffed into a pita pocket. Try stuffing it with crisp lettuce and a piece of thinly sliced cheese. Let your child pour on the dressing or eat it "naked."

Take a rolling pin to a slice of bread. Cut off the crusts. Spread peanut butter and jelly on the bread. Put a gherkin pickle on the edge of the bread. Roll up the bread and slice it into pinwheels. The pickle should be in the middle.

Spread peanut butter on the inside of a hot dog bun. Peel a banana and put it inside the bun. Presto!—a banana and peanut butter dog. (Send the banana in the lunch-box and let your child put bun and banana together.)

Take a large lettuce leaf. Plop your child's favorite salad mixture into the leaf. Roll it up. Wrap it tightly in plastic wrap if sending it to school.

Split a peach in two. Gently remove the pit. Fill the cavity with cottage cheese and raisins. Close up the peach. Wrap.

If you have more than one child brown-bagging it, mix and match their sandwiches.

Make a hero sandwich—processed meats, cold chicken, lettuce, sliced cheese and a little mustard. Instead of putting the sandwich in a gigantic hero-loaf, use a hot dog bun.

Peanut butter is a staple of childhood, although we all know children who'd rather clean their rooms than go near the stuff. But peanut butter can cause problems. It sticks to the roof of the mouth. If spread on white bread and gummed by a toddler, it can roll up into a nasty ball and cause choking.

Tips

- Wrap a slice of watermelon in foil and freeze overnight. Put at the bottom of the lunchbox. While defrosting, during the morning, the melon will keep the lunch cool and will taste refreshing at lunchtime.
- Freeze a tetra pack of juice. Wrap it in plastic. (As it defrosts it will sweat.) Put it at the bottom of the lunchbox.
- Freeze an individual-size container of yogurt. This too will keep the lunch cool as it defrosts.
- Invest in several wide-mouth thermoses.
- Trading is the name of the game. Give your child something to trade.
- Send a salad to school. Slice the top off a grapefruit. Scoop out the pulp. Mix some of the pulp with sliced grapes, strawberries, sliced melon, chopped apples sprinkled with lemon juice, chopped walnuts and a little commercially prepared low-fat mayonnaise. Put the salad into the grapefruit shell. Put the top of the grapefruit back on, wrap and send to school.
- To keep the sandwich filling from turning the bread into organic flannelet, spread margarine on both sides

of the sandwich. The idea here is to form a barrier between the bread and the filling.

- Homemade mayonnaise is wonderful. Use it everywhere except in your child's lunch, on a picnic or in a buffet that will be on display for a few hours. Use commercial mayonnaise instead. It keeps longer.

Snacks

Children under four years of age need to eat frequently throughout the day. On average, children under four will eat about six times a day, although some children will nibble up to ten or more times a day. At this young age, how often they eat is not as important as what they eat.

A normal day for a four-year-old would include breakfast, snack, lunch, snack, dinner and usually a light bedtime snack.

Considering the number of times a child snacks, a parent would be wise to take snacks seriously. Most snacks should provide nutrients and an appropriate number of calories. Fresh fruit, raw vegetables, cereal, trail mix (for children able to manage nuts) are perfect snack foods.

Some snack food, however, can be just plain fun.

GREEN POPCORN

2 tbsp butter	30 ml
4 cups popped corn	1 L
1 tbsp lime-flavored jelly powder	15 ml
salt to taste	

Melt butter and pour over corn. Toss. Sprinkle jelly powder and toss again.

To make pink popcorn, use strawberry-flavored jelly powder.

Nutty Popcorn

2 tbsp butter	30 ml
4 cups popped corn	1 L
6 oz peanuts	175 g
6 oz raisins	175 g
salt to taste	

Melt butter, mix with other ingredients and serve.

Square Popcorn

4 cups popped corn	1 L
1 cup peanut butter	250 ml
$\frac{1}{2}$ cup honey	125 ml

Melt peanut butter and honey together. Pour over popped corn. Put in 8-inch-square (20 cm), greased cake pan. Press popcorn down. Chill. Cut into squares.

Cheesy Popcorn

4 tbsp butter	60 ml
4 cups popped corn	1 L
$\frac{1}{2}$ cup grated Parmesan cheese	125 ml
salt to taste	

Melt butter and pour over warm popcorn. Mix salt with cheese and add to popcorn.

Gorp

If your older child is into after-school activities, you'll want to pack an after-school snack, particularly if the activities are sports. Children should not eat eight-hour-old sandwiches. (Peanut butter sandwiches are usually

OK, but egg salad sandwiches that have been sitting on stinky running shoes in a smelly locker should be tossed.) Pack a bag of gorp instead.

1 cup crunchy breakfast cereal	250 ml
a handful of raisins	
a handful of peanuts	
a few tbsp of sesame seeds	
chocolate bits (optional)	
coconut bits (optional)	

Send to school in a plastic jar.

Note: You can buy a variety of nut mixes in bulk bins. For the freshest product choose a store where a large number of people shop. Store the gorp in a jar.

SNAPPY CHEESE STICKS (PAM COLLACOTT)

These are tasty cold and terrific warm. Make them ahead and reheat.

$\frac{1}{2}$ cup grated sharp Cheddar cheese	125 ml
1 cup biscuit mix	250 ml
$\frac{1}{3}$ cup milk	75 ml
$\frac{1}{3}$ cup flour	75 ml
2 tbsp soft butter or margarine	30 ml

Add cheese to biscuit mix and stir in milk. Mix with fork until well blended. Roll out on lightly floured surface to form a rectangle. Spread butter over surface and sprinkle grated cheese over entire surface. Roll up like a jelly roll. Fold roll in half, flatten slightly, then roll into a rectangle 1/4-inch (1 cm) thick. Cut into narrow 1-inch

(2.5 cm) strips. Twist each strip as you place it on greased cookie sheet.

Bake at 450°F (230°C) for 6 to 8 minutes or until puffed and golden.

HOCKEY PUCKS
(Best served during the game.)

$2\frac{1}{2}$ cups corn flakes or Rice Krispies	625 ml
$\frac{1}{2}$ cup peanut butter	125 ml
$\frac{1}{4}$ cup honey	50 ml
1 tsp vanilla	5 ml

Pour corn flakes into bowl and let the children grind them down a little. Then mix all ingredients together. Shape into balls. Place on waxed paper and press into pucks. Chill.

CAMEMBERT CHEESE DIP
This is a wonderful way to introduce a new cheese.

1 camembert cheese round, skin intact
almond slivers (optional)
bread sticks (for dipping)

Break the skin of the cheese by making an X on the top. Place on microwave dish. Sprinkle almonds over the cheese. Microwave on high for 60 seconds or until the cheese starts to bubble up. Watch carefully. Dunk a bread stick in the sizzling cheese making sure it's not hot enough to burn a little mouth. Enjoy!

TOASTED PITA CHIPS

Open pita bread and separate the halves. Cut into wedges. Brush each wedge with light coating of olive oil. Sprinkle with dried parsley and basil, and other Italian herbs. Toast under broiler for 2 minutes or bake at 350°F (180°C) until crunchy (8 to 10 minutes). Let cool. Serve with dip or store in an air-tight container.

PESTO DIP

1 cup basil, chopped	250 ml
1 clove garlic	1
3 tbsp grated Parmesan cheese	45 ml
2 tsp lemon juice	10 ml
2 tsp olive oil	10 ml
1 cup sour cream	250 ml
1 cup plain yogurt	250 ml

Toasted slivered almonds or pine nuts may be added.

Blend together all ingredients except sour cream and yogurt. Stir in sour cream and yogurt. Serve.

KIDS WHO DIP (PATTI LOWSHAW)

1 cup sour cream	250 ml
1 cup mayonnaise	250 ml
1 tsp parsley flakes	5 ml
1 tsp green onion flakes	5 ml
2 tsp garlic salt	10 ml
$\frac{1}{2}$ tsp dill weed	2 ml
3 to 4 drops Tabasco	3 to 4

Mix together all ingredients and let sit for 2 hours or more before serving. Scoop out the middle of a round loaf of bread. Pour dip into the hollow of the bread and let the children dip away, using chunks of bread as dippers.

RAW VEGGIE DIP (PATTI LOWSHAW)

$\frac{1}{2}$ cup mayonnaise	125 ml
3 tbsp grated onion	45 ml
3 tbsp ketchup	45 ml
3 tbsp honey	45 ml
2 tbsp lemon juice	10 ml
1 tsp curry powder	5 ml

Combine all ingredients and let sit for at least 2 hours. Serve with a variety of raw veggies.

REFRIED BEAN DIP

14-oz can refried (or leftover) brown beans	400 ml
$\frac{1}{2}$ cup cream cheese	125 ml

Mix together.

Note: If your children like a little zip, add 2 tsp (10 ml) chili powder and a dash of garlic salt.

WON TON CHIPS

Separate won ton wrappers and cut into triangles. Lightly brush each shape with olive oil (optional) and bake for 4 minutes at 350°F (180°C) or until crispy. Serve with dip.

TORTILLA CHIPPIES

Cut 4 tortillas into 6 wedges. Spread on nonstick cookie sheet and toast for 5 minutes in 350°F (180°C) oven. Store in air-tight container. Serve with dip or eat like chips.

FRUITY DIP

Into one individual serving of plain yogurt, mix 1 tbsp (15 ml) of orange or raspberry juice concentrate. Sprinkle with poppy seeds (optional). Serve with slices of peach, strawberry, banana, pear, apple (give apples an ultra-thin coat of lemon juice to prevent them from turning brown).

AFTER-SCHOOL APPLE (MICROWAVE)

1 medium to large red apple	1
1 tbsp brown sugar	15 ml
1 tbsp raisins	15 ml

Cut top off apple. Set top aside. Scoop out as much of core as possible leaving a round, deep indentation. Pierce inside of apple with a knife. Stab outside skin of apple as well (to prevent it from exploding). Fill apple with brown sugar and raisins. Put top back on apple. Microwave on high for 1 minute or until brown sugar bubbles up and all but disappears into apple. Let cool for a minute before serving.

TOASTED SESAME SEED CHEESE

Spread sesame seeds on cookie sheet. Put under broiler for a few minutes. Shake. Do not burn. Let cool.

Cut up Cheddar cheese into $\frac{1}{4}$ x 1-inch (1 x 2.5 cm) strips. Press cheese down onto sesame seeds. Coat all sides. Wrap in plastic individually. Great for lunches.

· ·

"I stood in the grocery line behind a woman who had the audacity to comment on my grocery order. She pointed to a box of cereal that contained marshmallows and said, 'I would never feed my children that junk.' I had to laugh. Her basket was piled high with chips and cheesies and pop. I said that my kids didn't eat chips, but on Saturday nights, our video time, they were allowed to snack on silly-cereal. I'd prefer our silly-cereal to processed snacks anytime."

· ·

CEREAL BALLS

Mix honey and peanut butter with your child's favorite cereal. Add raisins, sesame seeds, sunflower seeds or any preferred nuts. Shape into little balls. Chill.

GOLF BALLS

2 to 3 oz cream cheese	60 to 75 g
2 tbsp peanut butter	30 ml
2 tbsp honey	30 ml
2 tbsp milk powder	30 ml
shredded coconut	

Mix first four ingredients. Shape into small balls and roll in shredded coconut.

CEREAL TOPPING

Top frozen yogurt with a mixture of honey, nuts and a favorite dried cereal.

NUTS & BOLTS

2 tbsp butter or margarine	30 ml
1 tbsp Worcestershire sauce	15 ml
$\frac{1}{2}$ tsp seasoning salt	2 ml
4 to 6 cups of all the cereals in your cupboard (Cheerios, Cap'n Crunch, Rice Chex, Shreddies, etc.) 1 to 1.5 L	
1 cup trail mix	250 ml
shake of garlic powder	

Melt butter in pan and mix in spices. Toss in cereals. Mix. Bake at 300°F (160°C) for 30 minutes. Stir twice during the cooking.

JUICE POPS

Use one $12\frac{1}{2}$-oz (355 ml) can of concentrated juice. Add half recommended amount of water. Fill popsicle tray and freeze. Or, use ice-cube tray and add popsicle sticks or plastic stirrers when almost frozen.

FRUITY POPS

$\frac{1}{2}$ cup strawberries	125 ml
2 tbsp frozen juice concentrate	30 ml
1 tbsp honey	15 ml
$\frac{1}{2}$ cup water	125 ml

Blend strawberries (or raspberries or blueberries) in food processor. Strain. Add water, juice concentrate and honey. Pour into popsicle molds. Makes 8 pops.

YOGURT POPS #1

Put favorite fruit-in-the-bottom yogurt in blender. Whirl for 1 minute or until liquefied. Pour into popsicle molds and freeze.

Or, substitute paper cups for popsicle molds. Insert sticks when almost frozen. When frozen, dip paper cups into water and quickly peel paper away from pop.

YOGURT POPS #2

1 banana	1
2 tbsp honey	30 ml
$\frac{1}{2}$ cup milk	125 ml
$\frac{1}{2}$ cup plain yogurt	125 ml

Whirl in blender and pour into molds. Makes about 8 pops.

CREAM POPS

$\frac{2}{3}$ cup milk	150 ml
$\frac{2}{3}$ cup peach yogurt	150 ml
1 small ripe peach, skinned and pitted	1
1 tsp honey (optional)	5 ml

Blend all ingredients until smooth. Poor into molds. Makes about 10 to 12 pops.

7

DINNER PLUS

Main Meals

Each of the following recipes was included after being tested and approved by children. Most recipes are simple and lightly spiced. They allow you a lot of leeway to substitute, add or subtract according to your child's preferences. The recipes have been tested using imperial measurements. Metric measurements may differ slightly.

There are no stews in this book. Not that stews aren't wonderful; it's just that most picky eaters need to recognize every single ingredient on their plates. Our sample stew recipes just didn't pass the picky eater palate test. (We tried, honestly!)

The recipes may seem a little lopsided. There are no recipes in this book for muffins and cakes, and few for chicken or burgers. Why? Few parents complained about their children rejecting fried chicken or a chocolate-chip muffin in favor of broccoli! The recipes in this book concentrate on salads and vegetables, but yes, there are lots of snacks and other tasty treats.

Finally, the recipes do not suggest the number of children served. We have no way of knowing just how much, if anything, children will eat.

Study the recipes with your children. Let them pick out a few to test. Visit the bookstore and pick up a few other recipe books together. Cuddle in with your child for a before-bedtime read with a recipe or food book. Well, why not? Not only will your child's reading skills improve, but you may find a new hobby.

JUNGLE SALAD (PAM COLLACOT)

1 apple, peeled and chopped	1
1 pineapple ring, chopped	1
1 banana, peeled and sliced	1
$\frac{1}{2}$ cup seedless grapes, halved	125 ml
$\frac{1}{4}$ cup peanuts (optional)	50 ml
$\frac{1}{2}$ cup fruit-flavored yogurt	125 ml
coconut, flaked (optional)	

Combine fruits in bowl. Stir in yogurt and gently mix. Sprinkle with coconut.

....

"I have a bowl tucked away in the cupboard. It's filled with ridiculous little trinkets like tiny paper umbrellas, plastic monkeys, a couple of farm animals, some soldiers, a plastic Batman and any number of swizzle sticks. Once in a while I decorate our plates with these little toys. The kids love it."

....

Note: Children should help in the preparation. If that's not possible, allow them to pour in their favorite fruit-flavored yogurt and mix. However, some children don't like their fruit "gunked up." For these, try serving the yogurt on the side as a dip.

SUMMER LIME FRUIT SALAD
Assorted fruits cut into dipping chunks.

strawberries	
blueberries	
honeydew melon	
grapes	
pineapple	
1 tsp poppy seeds (optional)	5 ml

Arrange on fruit plate. Sprinkle with poppy seeds, and serve with the following dip.

Dip

1 cup plain yogurt	250 ml
2 tbsp honey	30 ml
2 tsp lime juice (1 small lime)	10 ml
1 tsp grated lime peel	5 ml

Line a strainer with a paper towel and pour in yogurt. Put in fridge for 1 to 3 hours to drain. The yogurt will thicken. Add thickened yogurt to the remaining ingredients. (Discard the drained liquid.)

SALAD WITH QUICK FRUIT DRESSING

$\frac{1}{2}$ cup chopped iceberg lettuce	125 ml
$\frac{1}{2}$ cup chopped watercress	125 ml

Dressing: Blend together equal parts of orange juice concentrate and olive oil. Add vinegar to taste. Splash over greens and serve.

CARROT AND PINEAPPLE SALAD

8-oz can crushed pineapple with juice	227 ml
2 medium carrots, grated	2
$\frac{1}{2}$ cup raisins	125 ml

Mix all ingredients together. Serve on hot dogs, over iceberg lettuce or in a bowl on its own.

BAG SALAD

$\frac{1}{2}$ cup chopped lettuce	125 ml
1 tomato, chopped	1
3 tbsp shredded Cheddar cheese	45 ml
2 to 4 tbsp salad dressing	30 to 60 ml

Let the child put all ingredients in a plastic bag. Shake. Serve.

••

"I find it hard to let my kids help in the kitchen. I like to get things over with, get the job done. On the other hand, I have great fantasies about my kids making me breakfast in bed. (I did say the word 'fantasies.') My six- and nine-year-old have chosen several recipes that they can make by themselves. I helped the first time, supervised the second, and now only occasionally yell directions from the living room. Need I mention that the recipes *do not* call for flour, and although the kids do clean up, sorta, I don't complain."

••

ORANGE HEAD SALAD (TRINA TULK)

$\frac{1}{2}$ head of iceberg lettuce, torn into bits	$\frac{1}{2}$
1 tbsp each of favorite chopped vegetables (green or red pepper, carrots, mild onion, cucumber)	15 ml
2 to $2\frac{1}{2}$ tbsp mayonnaise	30 to 40 ml
2 tsp sugar	10 ml
1 cup grated mild Cheddar cheese	250 ml
$\frac{1}{4}$ lb homemade bacon bits	125 g

Layer the ingredients in this order: lettuce, chopped vegetables, mayonnaise, sugar sprinkled over mayonnaise, Cheddar, bacon bits.

This salad can be made ahead and kept in a cool place until dinner. Toss at the table.

Note: If you find the mayonnaise a tad too thick, thin it with a little milk, or mix $1\frac{1}{2}$ tbsp (20 ml) mayonnaise with $1\frac{1}{2}$ tbsp (20 ml) plain yogurt.

Use a glass bowl.

To make a smiling face, press an orange rind (the smile) against the glass bowl. Use carrot rounds for eyes and a slice of pickle for the nose. To make a second face, flip the orange rind (the frown) and press it on the opposite side of the bowl. Do this before layering the salad.

••

"My daughter nagged for a bag of chips. As usual I said no. She kept at it. I asked her, 'Why do you keep nagging me? You know nagging doesn't work.' At the dinner table that night I told her to eat her vegetables. I must have repeated myself twenty times and *still* she wouldn't eat her vegetables. She turned to me and said, 'Why do you keep nagging me? You know nagging doesn't work.'"

••

BROCCOLI TREES (CATHY MACDONALD)

1 head broccoli, broken into small bits	1
10 oz trail mix*	275 g
2 tbsp mayonnaise	30 ml
2 tsp sugar	10 ml
5 to 8 strips bacon, cooked crisp and crumbled	5 to 8
$\frac{1}{2}$ medium mild onion, diced	$\frac{1}{2}$

* Your favorite nut combination of trail mix will do but make sure that the mix *does not* contain chocolate chips.

Mix all ingredients together and store until serving time in fridge. Keeps for several hours. Great in a lunchbox.

••

"My husband had lost his job and we were having a tough time financially. I decided that my family needed a good, cheap, laugh. After dinner I dimmed the lights and brought out a candle-lit, store-bought birthday cake. I sang happy birthday to the dog. My husband and children were in stitches. They didn't notice that the cake was a two-day-old special or that the candles had already been used. That was twenty-two years ago. Once in a while, and out of the blue, I still buy a birthday cake for the dog."

••

Yo-Slaw

2 cups shredded cabbage	500 ml
$\frac{1}{2}$ cup sliced celery	125 ml
1 apple, peeled, cored and diced	1
$\frac{1}{2}$ cup raisins	125 ml
$\frac{1}{2}$ cup grapes	125 ml
1 orange, peeled and cut into chunks	1
1 carrot, peeled and sliced	1
1 small individual tub yogurt with fruit bottom	175 g
2 tbsp mayonnaise	30 ml
poppy seeds (optional)	

Mix all ingredients together and serve. Will keep several hours in the refrigerator.

BROCCOLI AND CHEESE SAUCE (JAYNE STAFFORD)

Steam broccoli flowerets until tender and bright green.

Sauce

$\frac{1}{4}$ cup butter	50 ml
$\frac{1}{4}$ cup flour	50 ml
2 cups 2% milk	500 ml
1 cup grated Cheddar cheese	250 ml

Melt butter in saucepan. Whisk in flour and stir for 2 or 3 minutes. Over medium heat, gradually stir in milk and bring to boil. Reduce heat, add cheese and stir until melted. Pour over broccoli.

CHEESE ZUCCHINI

4 small zucchini	4
1 to 2 tbsp bread crumbs	15 to 30 ml
$\frac{1}{2}$ cup shredded Swiss cheese	125 ml
1 to 2 tbsp chopped parsley	15 to 30 ml
1 to 2 tbsp butter	15 to 30 ml
salt and pepper to taste	

Steam whole zucchini until tender but not mushy. Cut in half lengthwise. Preheat oven to 350°F (180°C). Place zucchini in prepared baking pan with cut side up. Gently scoop out a little of the zucchini meat to form a small hollow. Spoon in bread crumbs and then cheese followed by parsley. Sprinkle with a little salt (optional) and pepper. Dot with butter. Bake for 30 minutes.

MINI STIR-FRY

2 tbsp oil	30 ml
1 medium zucchini, cubed	1
1 cup broccoli, chopped	250 ml
2 corn, shucked	2
soya sauce (optional)	

Heat oil in pan or wok. Add vegetables and toss for 5 minutes. Vegetables should be crisp. Add soya sauce only at your child's request.

Note: A simple stir-fry, without soya sauce, bean sprouts or spices, is often an appealing introduction to a more complicated stir-fry. Start with three favorite and familiar vegetables and build up from there. Add shrimp, meat and so on as your child becomes accustomed to a medley of foods. You may now also find that your child may more readily accept stews or other meals that combine foods with sauces.

LISA'S CHICKEN WINGS (LISA VALERIOTE)

2 dozen chicken wings	24
$\frac{1}{2}$ cup soya sauce	125 ml
2 oz white sugar	50 g
1 cup water	250 ml
1 tbsp vegetable oil	15 ml
$\frac{1}{2}$ cup orange juice	125 ml
$\frac{3}{4}$ tsp ginger	3 ml
$\frac{3}{4}$ tsp garlic powder	3 ml

Cut tips off wings and arrange on baking dish. Mix together soya sauce, sugar, water, oil, orange juice, ginger and garlic powder. Pour liquid over chicken. Put into baking dish. Bake at 350°F (180°C) for $1^{1}/_{2}$ hours. Baste and turn as needed.

Alternative: To crisp wings, put under a hot broiler for 3 minutes on each side (watch them closely). Or, put on the barbecue for 5 minutes. Serve with a Blue Cheese Dip.

Dip: Mash 2 oz (60 g) of blue cheese with 3 to 4 tbsp (45 to 60 ml) of mayonnaise, a pinch of dry mustard and a dash of Tabasco sauce. If the dip is too strong for the children, mix in a little plain yogurt or sour cream. (Better yet, have the children do the mixing and taste-testing as they go along. An adult should handle the Tabasco sauce.)

BEEF KABOBS

6 tbsp soya sauce (Japanese, salt reduced preferred)	90 ml
12-oz can pineapple chunks	341 ml
$\frac{1}{2}$ tbsp ground fresh ginger (more if desired)	7 ml
1 clove garlic, crushed	1
1 lb beef sirloin, cut into bite-size chunks	500 g
1 green pepper, chopped into bite-size chunks	1

Pour soya sauce in a bowl and add juice from can of pineapple, ginger, garlic and beef. Marinate the beef for 1 to 2 hours in mixture. Remove beef chunks, reserving marinade.

Thread beef, pineapple and green pepper onto skewers. Barbecue or grill, basting with marinade.

Note: Add different vegetables such as mushrooms, tomato or onion chunks as your child develops and expands her tastes.

If corn on the cob is a favorite, chop a cob into three equal-size chunks. Thread corn, meat, corn, meat onto skewer. Brush corn lightly with olive oil before barbecuing or grilling.

Tip: Soak wooden skewers for several hours before using. Do not let young children handle the skewers (they have a way of fencing with them). Remove the meat and vegetables from the skewers before serving.

PIZZA PROJECT

Pizza tip: Whether you use an English muffin or prepared mini-pizza shell, brush the surface with an ultra-thin layer of oil before adding any toppings. This will prevent the dough from becoming too mushy and give your creation that certain pizza-parlor finish.

6 English muffins, sliced in half (2 halves per child)	
4 tbsp oil	60 ml
1 small jar prepared spaghetti sauce (see Dot's Spaghetti Sauce page 118)	
little dishes of oregano, basil, chives	
shredded cheese (Cheddar, Mozzarella)	
pepperoni (optional)	
green pepper (optional)	
onions (optional)	

Preheat oven to 350°F (180°C). Bake for 5 minutes or until cheese is melted.

The children can choose their own toppings. Try offering at least one new topping every time you serve up mini-pizzas. Examples: cooked shrimp, feta cheese, pineapple chunks, tomatoes and so on.

Note: Encourage children to smell and touch the seasonings. They may prefer to pass them up this time.

•••

"We never eat out. I like my own cooking. Just the thought of eating Japanese or Thai food gives me the shivers. And I don't like any type of fish, raw or cooked. I like plain, simple food—meat and potatoes. And no, I wouldn't consider my children picky eaters. They like meat and potatoes, too."

•••

THE SALAD BAR

•••

"Do you want any salad?" The question was directed to a six-year-old. "I'd rather take a bath," was the reply.

•••

Your child does not "like" salad. But you take him out to one of those all-you-can-eat salad bars and he eats his head off. Parents' Credo: DON'T FIGHT IT. BEAT IT.

MAKE A MINI SALAD BAR

Put all items in separate bowls. Give each child her own plate and try, oh try, to say nothing when she dumps globs of dressing on one pathetic green leaf.

Suggestions: shredded carrots, broccoli flowerets, tuna chunks, thawed frozen vegetables, sliced hard-boiled eggs, Cheddar cheese chunks, cooked chicken chunks, salami and ham strips, canned baby corn, peanuts, raisins, chopped iceberg lettuce. Offer two types of dressing for that "restaurant" touch.

Note: Serve at a birthday party for the nines and up.

SALAD IN A POCKET

1 pita pocket	
mixture of shredded iceberg lettuce, red cabbage and carrots	
1 slice of favorite hard cheese (Mozzarella, Cheddar, etc.)	

Stuff all into pita pocket and wrap.

Tahini dressing:

$\frac{1}{4}$ cup tahini (sesame butter)	50 ml
$\frac{1}{4}$ cup water	50 ml
$\frac{1}{2}$ tsp minced garlic	2 ml
1 tsp lemon juice	5 ml
salt to taste	

Whirl in a blender.

A child can pour the dressing into the pita at lunchtime. (Pack the dressing in a small container. Send several napkins.)

BABY WALDORF

$\frac{1}{2}$ lb green grapes, seeded and halved	250 g
$\frac{1}{2}$ lb red grapes, seeded and halved	250 g
1 red apple, cored and cut into chunks	1
1 green apple, cored and cut into chunks	1

$\frac{1}{4}$ red onion, finely chopped	$\frac{1}{4}$
squish of lemon over the apples	
sprinkle of walnuts, chopped	
2 to 3 tbsp mayonnaise	25 to 45 ml

Mix. (Mixture will keep in fridge for an hour or so.)

It's pretty, it's simple and chances are, if you let the children add all the ingredients, they *may* even eat it.

Note: If your child wants her grapes "plain," serve the mayonnaise on the side. It may be enough to have her taste the fruits in combination.

STUFF YOUR OWN POTATO

1 tbsp butter (or less)	15 ml
2 potatoes	2
$\frac{1}{4}$ cup shredded Cheddar cheese	50 ml
salt and pepper to taste	

Prick skin of potato and bake in 450°F (230°C) oven for 40 minutes or until potatoes are tender. Scoop out half the filling. Brush insides of potato skins with butter. Sprinkle with salt and pepper. Mix potato pulp with Cheddar cheese and restuff potato skin. Bake at 350°F (180°C) for another 5 to 10 minutes or until cheese is melted. Should serve 4 children.

Toppings: lump fish caviar (not too expensive); capers; bacon bits; raisins; sliced bananas; pine nuts.

"If I put it on his plate he won't eat it. If I let him help himself he'll try it. I've come to the conclusion that the more control my son has over his food, the more likely he is to eat. Oh, and candy is not one of the offered choices. I've kept a little power."

Zucchini Boats

Thirty mobiles, created by thirty children, dangled from the classroom ceiling. Each mobile had different pieces of paper that read "I hate..." "I love..." "I dislike..." and so on. Under the "I hate" category, twenty-eight out of the thirty children listed mushrooms as their favorite "hate."

This recipe calls for mushrooms. Our adult testers loved it but their children had mixed opinions. We included it in the end because it's so easy to substitute almost any other vegetable for the mushrooms and because there are a few children who really do like mushrooms.

2 medium-size zucchini	2
$\frac{1}{2}$ lb mushrooms, sliced or 4 medium carrots, diced	250 g
1 medium mild onion, chopped	1
2 tbsp oil	30 ml
1 bunch parsley, chopped	1
$\frac{1}{2}$ cup Parmesan cheese	125 ml

Cut zucchini in half lengthwise, scoop out seeds. Steam for 5 minutes, until firm but not mushy. Gently fry mushrooms, onion and parsley in oil until soft. Fill zucchini boats with mixture, top with Parmesan cheese and put under broiler for 3 minutes or until cheese has melted.

Alternative: Fill zucchini boats with mashed potatoes and chopped parsley instead of mushrooms and onions. Top with Parmesan cheese and put under broiler.

POTATO WEDGES

5 baking potatoes	5
$\frac{1}{3}$ cup vegetable oil or butter	75 ml
juice of $\frac{1}{2}$ lemon	

Wash potatoes and cut into wedge-shaped slices, keeping skin on. Use oil or butter to grease the pan. Arrange potatoes on baking tray. Drizzle with lemon juice, salt and pepper. Bake at 450°F (230°C) for 45 minutes. Stir occasionally.

••

"My kids woke up to a 'Backwards Day.' I woke them up by sitting on a bed and reading them a story. Breakfast was mini-portions of pork chops, vegetables, potatoes and salad. Lunch was—well lunch! Dinner was bacon, eggs, sausages—the works. My kids thought it was great. My wife, on the other hand, thought I needed my head read."
••

POTATO PIZZA

1 large potato	1
$\frac{1}{2}$ clove garlic, crushed	$\frac{1}{2}$
5 tbsp pizza sauce	75 ml
1 tomato, thinly sliced	1

$\frac{1}{2}$ small green pepper, slivered	$\frac{1}{2}$
5 tbsp grated Mozzarella cheese	75 ml

Prick potato and bake in 450°F (230°C) oven for 40 minutes or until tender but firm. Slice into $\frac{1}{2}$-inch (1 cm) circles, leaving peel on. Spread thin coating of garlic over each potato circle. Top each circle with 1 tbsp (15 ml) pizza sauce, slice of tomato, slivers of green pepper (or favorite vegetable). Sprinkle with Mozzarella cheese, and bake in 350°F (180°C) oven for 10 minutes or until potato pizzas are heated and cheese is melted.

Alternative: Cover potato slice with salsa sauce, chopped onion and Cheddar cheese. Bake.

Note: You can use left-over baked potatoes for this recipe or cook a few extra and reserve.

SPINACH SQUARES

This is one of those recipes that children shouldn't like but they usually do. Try serving it at your next play group.

3 eggs	3
1 cup flour (regular or whole wheat)	250 ml
1 cup milk	250 ml
2 cups shredded sharp cheese	500 ml
4 cups chopped raw spinach	1 L
salt and pepper to taste	

Mix all ingredients. Pour into greased 9 x 13 inch (23 x 32 cm) pan. Bake at 350°F (180°C) for 20 to 25 minutes, until lightly golden. Cut into squares and serve hot or cold.

LIKABLE LIVER

1 lb calves' liver	500 g
1 cup milk (or to cover)	250 ml
1 onion	1
$\frac{1}{4}$ cup ketchup	50 ml
1 tbsp white vinegar	15 ml
1 tbsp Worcestershire sauce	15 ml
1 tbsp brown sugar	15 ml
1 tsp prepared mustard	5
$\frac{1}{4}$ tsp chili powder	2

Soak liver for a few hours, or overnight, in milk. Drain. (Discard milk.) Cut liver into bite-size pieces. Steam onion until soft. Put onion and liver in baking dish. Mix remaining ingredients together and pour over liver. Cover and bake for 30 minutes at 350°F (180°C).

VEGETABLE LASAGNA

1 medium eggplant	1
2 medium zucchini	2
$\frac{1}{2}$ lb spinach	250g
pepper to taste	
1 $\frac{1}{2}$ cups prepared spaghetti sauce	375 ml
1 $\frac{1}{2}$ cups cottage cheese	375 ml
8 oz Mozzarella cheese slices	250 g
1 tomato, sliced	1
3 to 4 tbsp grated Parmesan cheese	45 to 50 ml

Peel and slice eggplant and zucchini into ¹/₂-inch-thick (2 cm) circles. Steam for 3 minutes. Add spinach to steamer and steam for 2 more minutes. Pepper vegetables, then spread thin layer of sauce over bottom of lasagna pan. Spread ¹/₃ of steamed vegetables over the sauce. Layer half of cottage cheese, then layer ¹/₃ of Mozzarella cheese slices. Next spread ¹/₃ of sauce.

Repeat—vegetables, cottage cheese, Mozzarella, sauce. Spread sliced tomato over top and sprinkle with Parmesan cheese. Bake at 350°F (180°C) for 35 to 45 minutes, or until sauce is bubbling.

Note: Experiment by adding your child's favorite steamed vegetables to the lasagna.

MUFFIN POTATOES

5 potatoes, peeled	5
2 tbsp butter	30 ml
¼ cup flour	50 ml
1 cup shredded Cheddar cheese	250 ml
2 eggs	2
2 tsp baking powder	10 ml
pepper to taste	
1 tsp minced garlic	5 ml
5 tbsp grated Parmesan cheese	75 ml

Boil potatoes and mash, mixing in butter. Add flour, Cheddar cheese, lightly beaten eggs, baking powder, pepper and garlic. Divide mixture into well-greased muffin cups. Sprinkle with Parmesan cheese. Bake at 375°F (190°C) for 35 minutes.

APPLE JUICE PORK

4 pork chops	4
2 cups apple juice	500 ml
2 tsp curry powder	10 ml
$\frac{1}{4}$ tsp turmeric	1 ml
$\frac{1}{2}$ tsp ginger	2 ml
1 tbsp dry mustard	15 ml
2 small potatoes, sliced	2
2 carrots, sliced	2
1 cup broccoli, chopped	1
1 small onion, chopped	1
1 zucchini	1

Marinate pork chops in half the apple juice for 1 to 2 hours. Remove chops and discard juice. Brown chops in a little oil in a skillet. Add to pan remaining apple juice, all spices, potatoes, carrots, broccoli and onion. Simmer for 20 minutes. Add zucchini. Simmer for 10 more minutes. Serve with rice or noodles.

Note: In a pinch, substitute ginger ale for apple juice.

FOOD FOR TOADS (EVELYN RAAB)

1 lb frozen tofu, thawed	500 g
2 tbsp vegetable oil	30 ml
$\frac{1}{2}$ cup chopped onion	125 ml
$\frac{1}{2}$ cup chopped green pepper	125 ml
1 clove garlic, minced	1

1 cup tomato sauce	250 ml
1 tsp Worcestershire sauce	5 ml
$\frac{1}{2}$ tsp chili powder	2 ml
$\frac{1}{2}$ tsp salt	2 ml
pinch of cayenne pepper	
10 taco shells	10
Toppings: shredded lettuce, chopped tomatoes, taco sauce	

Squeeze excess water from thawed tofu and tear into small bits. Heat oil in large skillet and add crumbled tofu. Cook for a few minutes or until golden brown. Add onions, green peppers and garlic. Sauté about 5 minutes. Add rest of ingredients and simmer for 10 more minutes. Spoon into taco shells and top with usual accompaniments.

MEATY TACOS

Small children have very sensitive taste buds. This recipe is designed for children. As they get used to spice, add cayenne pepper and extra chili powder.

1 lb lean ground beef	500 g
1 clove garlic, mashed	1
$\frac{1}{2}$ onion, chopped finely (optional)	$\frac{1}{2}$
$7\frac{1}{2}$-oz can tomato paste	213 ml
1 tbsp dry mustard	15 ml
2 tbsp chili powder (or less)	30 ml
8 to 10 taco shells	8 to 10

Brown ground beef with garlic and onion. Stir in tomato paste and all spices and simmer for 10 to 20 minutes. Spoon into taco shells.

Toppings: sour cream (use liberally if sauce is too spicy); shredded Cheddar cheese; shredded lettuce; diced tomatoes; chopped green and red pepper; taco sauce (prepared).

Alternative: Here's the lazy way. Brown meat. Take package of prepared taco mix (the seasoning mix) and add to meat. Mix in one small can tomato paste, pinch cayenne pepper, 2 tsp (10 ml) dry mustard. Spoon into taco shells. Presto! The best tacos in the neighborhood.

Note: Taco shells break easily. Small children may prefer soft tortillas.

Or, instead of using taco shells, choose the large, very crisp outer leaves of an iceberg lettuce. Let the children drop their taco mixture in the lettuce leaves and roll. The leaves are cool and delicious next to the spicy taco mixture.

TREES IN THE FOREST

Imagine serving broccoli, asparagus, mashed potato and peas at a birthday party. Now imagine all the party guests running home and demanding that their parents do the same!

4 potatoes, peeled	4
3 tbsp milk	45 ml
1 to 2 tbsp butter	15 to 30 ml
10 broccoli "trees" including "trunks"	10
10 asparagus spears	10
$\frac{1}{2}$ cup frozen peas	125 ml

2 cups shredded Cheddar cheese, loosely packed	500 ml
salt and pepper to taste	
sprigs of parsley	

Boil and mash potatoes with milk and butter. Season with salt and pepper. Spread mashed potatoes evenly over the bottom of square, 2-inch-deep (5 cm) pan. Steam broccoli and asparagus spears for 5 minutes. Add peas for the last 2 minutes. Vegetables *must* be crunchy! Do not over-steam. Make a winding "road" with peas on top of mashed potatoes. Stick broccoli "trees" in mashed potatoes on one side of the "road" and asparagus "trees" on the other side. Sprinkle Cheddar cheese over entire forest and cover with foil. Bake at 350°F (190°C) for 15 minutes.

Decorate with parsley "bushes."

Alternative: Choose a large deep dish. Surround the forest with great "rock boulders" (Treasure Meat Balls, see below). Just before serving, make a "pool" in the middle of the forest for your favorite meat-ball spaghetti sauce.

Go nuts: To create a winter scene, use shredded Mozzarella cheese instead of Cheddar. To create a Saturn moonscape, used mashed turnip instead of potatoes. What ideas do your children have?

TREASURE MEAT BALLS

1 lb lean ground beef	500 g
1 egg, lightly beaten	1
½ cup finely chopped onion	125 ml
½ cup bread crumbs	125 ml

$\frac{1}{4}$ to $\frac{1}{2}$ cup milk	50 to 125 ml
1 tsp fine herbs	5 ml
$\frac{1}{4}$ cup canned pineapple, drained and finely chopped	50 ml

Mix together and form into 1-inch (2 cm) meat balls. Arrange on cookie sheet. Bake in 375°F (190°C) oven for 15 minutes. Turn once.

FETTUCINI

6 to 8 oz fettucini or spaghetti	150 to 250 g
2 tbsp butter	30 ml
2 tbsp flour	30 ml
$1\frac{1}{2}$ cups milk	375 ml
1 cup cream	250 ml
$\frac{1}{4}$ tsp salt (or less)	1 ml
$\frac{1}{4}$ tsp white pepper	1 ml
$\frac{1}{8}$ tsp ground red pepper flakes or pinch of cayenne	.5 ml
$1\frac{1}{2}$ cups grated Parmesan cheese	375 ml

Cook noodles until firm. Combine butter and flour in pan, heating until butter melts. Add milk and bring to boil, stirring constantly. Simmer for 5 minutes. Stir often. Add cream, salt, white pepper, red pepper and finally cheese. Mix with pasta. Taste and toss in extra pepper if needed.

Note: This is a very heavy dish but few children, once past the "where's-the-tomato-sauce" stage, can resist it.

Alternative: Here's a speedy version without the cream. Chop onions and bacon. Fry until onions are soft and bacon crisp. Boil pasta and put it into the still-warm frying pan. Working quickly, add one lightly beaten egg. Stir. Toss in 1 cup (250 ml) Parmesan cheese. Keep tossing. Add salt and pepper to taste. If it gets too thick, add a little milk.

Dot's Spaghetti Sauce

Spaghetti—it's a food group, ask any child. And it disguises a multitude of "good-for-you" foods.

Sauce

1 lb lean hamburger meat	500 g
1 large onion, diced	1
28-oz can tomatoes (stewed tomatoes work well too)	796 ml
$7\frac{1}{2}$-oz can tomato sauce	213 ml
1 can concentrated tomato soup	1
2 tbsp sugar	30 ml
1 tbsp crushed garlic	15 ml
$\frac{1}{2}$ tsp of paprika	2 ml
$\frac{1}{2}$ tsp curry powder	2 ml
dash of Tabasco sauce	
pepper to taste	

Fry meat until brown. Add remaining ingredients and simmer for 1 hour, stirring occasionally. Serve over cooked spaghetti.

Adult Options: Add mushrooms, diced green pepper and crushed red pepper.

Here's a tip: keep a jar of sauce in the fridge at all times. Plop it on toast, mix it in with any pasta, add it to soups. There are any number of last-minute meals you can make.

Note: We tried out several spaghetti-sauce recipes on our "test" children. This one won out, although not all the parents agreed. Perhaps it appealed to children because of the familiar tomato soup flavor that hovered in the background.

SPAGHETTI PIE

4 to 6 oz spaghetti	125 to 150 g
1 $\frac{1}{2}$ cups spaghetti sauce (tomato)	375 ml
1 egg, lightly beaten	1
2 tbsp oil	30 ml
$\frac{1}{2}$ onion, chopped	$\frac{1}{2}$
$\frac{1}{2}$ tsp (or less) black pepper	2 ml or less
1 cup cottage cheese	250 ml
4 to 6 slices Mozzarella cheese	4 to 6
4 tbsp grated Parmesan cheese	60 ml

Cook spaghetti in large pot *al dente* (firm). Heat oil and add onion. Fry until soft. Mix cooked pasta with onion and pepper. Add egg to mixture and continue mixing. Lightly oil cake pan or coat with nonstick spray.

To assemble pie: Put half of spaghetti in pan. Pour half of spaghetti sauce over the noodles. Spread cottage cheese over sauce. Spread half of Mozzarella cheese over cottage cheese. Cover with rest of spaghetti. Use up remaining sauce to cover the top. Sprinkle Parmesan cheese over tomato sauce.

Bake at 350°F (180°C) for 20 to 25 minutes or until sides are bubbling. Cut pie with pizza knife and serve.

ZIPPY TOMATO SAUCE AND SPAGHETTI

This is a very light sauce that can be made in minutes and left to simmer. Children who normally balk at the heavier spaghetti sauces may prefer this one.

3 tbsp olive oil	45 ml
28-oz can tomatoes	796 ml
1 small white onion, chopped	1
1 bay leaf	1
1 tbsp basil (or to taste)	15 ml
pepper to taste	

Heat oil in pan. Mash tomatoes in oil. Add chopped onion, bay leaf, basil and pepper. Simmer on low heat for half an hour. Remove bay leaf before serving.

Toss cooked spaghetti in sauce and sprinkle with Parmesan cheese.

SAM'S CHICKEN CUTLETS

4 precooked chicken cutlets*	4
8 tbsp Zippy Tomato Sauce or Dot's Spaghetti Sauce	120 ml
4 slices Mozzarella cheese	4

*Coat deboned chicken breasts with mixture of bread-crumbs, chopped parsley and herbs. Fry in nonstick skillet until brown on both sides. Freeze. Keep on hand for speedy meals.

Place precooked chicken cutlets on nonstick cookie sheet. Cover each cutlet with spaghetti sauce. Top with slices of Mozzarella cheese. Heat at 350°F (180°C) for 5 minutes or until cheese is bubbling.

Note: Homemade salsa may be substituted for spaghetti sauce.

••

"Tuesday nights are the worst. My husband is a Cub Scout Leader, my son is a Cub. I am a Brownie Leader and my daughter is a Brownie. My husband and I both work full-time. Picture the scene of flying uniforms, meals-on-the-fly and blue air. Dinner? ... Oh *please*."

••

CHICKEN DRUMBITS

Children are very often overwhelmed by the sheer size of food. Even a mere chicken drumstick can look daunting. Picture the drumstick of a 30-pound (13.5 kg) turkey balancing on your plate and you'll get some idea of just how big an ordinary chicken drumstick can look to a 45-pound (18.5 kg) child.

If your child is old enough to handle bones, opt for the "legs" of chicken wings. Take a chicken wing, break it in half at the joint and discard the tip. Peel back the skin. Make small cuts around the "leg" and push the meat up to the top of the bone. Now you have a cute little "drumstick" that really is kid-size.

1 tbsp paprika	15 ml
$\frac{1}{3}$ cup whole-wheat flour	75 ml

1 tbsp fine herbs (any combination of dried basil, parsley, oregano, thyme and rosemary)	15 ml
12 drumbits	12

Put flour and spices in a plastic bag. Add the drumbits two at a time and shake to coat evenly. Put drumbits on nonstick cookie sheet and bake at 425°F (220°C) for 15 minutes. Turn and bake for another 15 minutes.

Serve as finger food with salsa as a dip.

Or, mix cooked wings with 1 cup (250 ml) spaghetti sauce. Put wings in baking dish and reheat in the oven at 350°F (180°C) for 10 more minutes. Serve with favorite pasta.

PINK SOUP

3 large beets	3
2 tbsp lemon juice	30 ml
2 cups chicken stock	500 ml
1 can concentrated tomato soup (or substitute 1 cup (250 ml) meatless, canned spaghetti sauce)	
sour cream (to make it pink)	

Cook beets in enough water to cover. Once you can smell them (about 10 minutes) plunge them in cold water, lop off the tops and bottoms and slip off the skins. Chop into pieces. Cover chopped beets in 6 cups (1.5 L) of fresh water. Add lemon juice, chicken stock, tomato soup and cook for 20 minutes. Cool a little, then whirl in blender until smooth. Reheat. Swirl in sour cream to make a design.

GREEN SOUP (AND HAM)

2 lb broccoli	1 kg
1 bunch watercress	1
2 cups chicken stock	500 ml
2 cups milk	500 ml
$\frac{1}{2}$ tsp garlic powder	2 ml
white pepper to taste	
1 cup cooked ham chunks	250 ml

Steam broccoli and watercress until tender. Puree broccoli and watercress in batches in food processor or blender with stock, milk and spices. Return to stove and simmer for 20 minutes. Add ham chunks, or serve ham chunks alongside soup.

GREEN POTATOES (AND HAM)

2 large baking potatoes	2
1 lb broccoli	500 g
1 cup cooked ham, diced	250 ml
$\frac{1}{2}$ to 1 cup grated Cheddar cheese	125 to 250 ml
1 scallion, chopped	1

Bake potatoes for 1 hour at 400°F (200°C) or until done. Steam broccoli until soft. Cut potatoes in half and scoop out pulp, leaving the skin intact. Mash potato and broccoli together and mix in diced ham. Sprinkle with cheese and return to 350°F (180°C) oven for 10 minutes.

Mom's Chicken Soup

1 chicken carcass (leftovers)	1
1 medium onion, sliced	1
1 carrot, sliced	1
4 tbsp fresh parsley	60 ml
1 tsp poultry seasoning (more to taste)	5 ml
$\frac{1}{2}$ tsp pepper to taste	2 ml
1 cup minute rice (optional)	250 ml
1 chicken bullion cube (optional)	1

Put carcass in small pot (chicken should touch all sides). Add water (to cover), onion, carrot, half the chopped parsley and the seasonings. Simmer for 2 hours. Strain. Put broth in fridge for 10 hours or overnight. Skim off fat. Add remaining parsley, rice, and if necessary, boullion cube. Heat for 5 minutes or until rice is tender. Serve.

Grandma was right, chicken soup really does help ward off the common cold. Warm chicken soup helps loosen mucus and clears the head. There's a catch—the soup must be homemade. Canned or dried soups contain too much salt, which actually dries up the body.

Cool Red and Green Summer Soup

1 medium cantaloupe
1 medium honeydew melon
$\frac{1}{2}$ cup (125 ml) plain yogurt or sour cream
or 4 tbsp (60 ml) french vanilla ice cream

Peel and cut melons into chunks. Place cantaloupe chunks in blender. Whirl. Clean blender. Put honeydew melon chunks in blender. Whirl. Pour purees into two separate jugs. Take jugs, one in each hand, and pour into the same bowl from opposite sides. Half the bowl will be green, half red.

Plop 1 tbsp (15 ml) of plain yogurt or vanilla ice cream in the middle of the soup.

(Yeild: 4 individual servings)

Alternative: Clean, slice and sugar 1 cup (250 ml) of fresh strawberries. Put strawberries into blender. Puree. With a spoon, gently plop pureed strawberry sauce into soup to make giant red dots.

••

"My ten-year-old came up to me and said, 'You know, you haven't said one nice thing to me all day.' He was right. He then said that he wanted to be treated like a guest for the evening. Well why not? He left the house and a few minutes later I opened the door to my dinner guest. I took his coat, offered him a drink. (He asked for pop—smart kid.) During dinner we had a wonderful conversation (the first time in years). I didn't correct his table manners because he behaved like a guest and one doesn't correct a guest. After dinner we played a board game and then he donned his coat, bade me goodnight, and walked out the door. A moment later my grinning ten-year-old reappeared."

••

FRUITCREAM

Mix 1 cup (250 ml) of ice cream with 1 tbsp (15 ml) frozen concentrated orange juice. Add chopped mini-chunks of an orange. Spoon into an ice-cream cone and top with granola.

To dress it up as birthday party fare, heat up a bar of solid chocolate in a double boiler. Mix melted chocolate with 4 tbsp (60 ml) of granola and top fruit ice cream.

THE PEANUT BUTTER, CHOCOLATE-PEANUT-BUTTER SUPER-DUPER COOKIE (HEATHER MORTON)

$\frac{1}{4}$ cup butter	50 ml
$\frac{1}{4}$ cup shortening	50 ml
$\frac{1}{2}$ cup peanut butter	125 ml
$\frac{1}{2}$ cup white sugar	125 ml
$\frac{1}{2}$ cup brown sugar	125 ml
1 egg	1
1 tsp vanilla	5 ml
1 cup flour	250 ml
$\frac{1}{2}$ tsp baking soda	2 ml
$\frac{1}{4}$ tsp salt	1 ml
$\frac{3}{4}$ cup chocolate chips	175 ml
$\frac{1}{2}$ cup peanut butter chips	125 ml

Cream together butter, shortening and peanut butter in large bowl. Mix in sugars and continue creaming mixture. Mix in egg and vanilla. Beat until smooth. Add flour, baking soda and salt. Mix in chocolate and peanut-butter chips and drop by the teaspoon onto greased baking sheet. Flatten just a little with back of spoon.

Bake at 350°F (180°C) for 9 to 10 minutes. Makes about 4 dozen cookies.

Tip: Remove cookies from pan as soon as they come out of the oven.

HEATHER'S CHOCOLATE-CHIP COWBOYS (HEATHER MORTON)

$\frac{1}{2}$ cup shortening	125 ml
$\frac{1}{2}$ cup sugar	125 ml
$\frac{1}{4}$ cup brown sugar	50 ml
1 egg	1
1 tsp vanilla	5 ml
1 cup flour	250 ml
$\frac{1}{4}$ tsp salt	1 ml
$\frac{1}{2}$ tsp baking soda	2 ml
1 cup large chocolate chips	250 ml
$\frac{1}{4}$ to $\frac{1}{2}$ cup chopped walnuts	50 to 125 ml

In a bowl, cream together shortening, sugars, egg and vanilla. Mix until fluffy. Mix in flour, salt and baking soda until well combined. Stir in chocolate chips and chopped walnuts. Drop by the teaspoonful onto greased tray. Bake at 350°F (180°C) for 9 minutes.

Tip: Substitute M&M's or Smarties for chocolate chips for special birthday cookies.

Puppy Chew (Mary Ella McGraw)

$\frac{1}{2}$ box Crispex cereal (Shreddies or similar dry cereal may be substituted)	$\frac{1}{2}$
1 cup peanut butter	250 ml
1 cup chocolate chips	250 ml
$\frac{1}{4}$ cup margarine	50 ml
2 cups icing sugar (or more)	500 ml

Pour cereal into roasting pan and warm in 350°F (180°C) oven. Pour peanut butter, chocolate chips and margarine into pot and melt on medium-low heat. Pour peanut butter mixture over cereal and stir gently. Put icing sugar in a brown paper grocery bag. Pour coated cereal into bag and shake until the pieces have separated and are coated in sugar.

Tuna Pocket Melt

This is a favorite with many children. Omitted are the "green things" such as green onions, relish, chopped pickles and so on. And take out the "red things" such as chopped red pepper and sprinkles of paprika. By all means dice them all up and add them to the recipe if your child is red and green tolerant.

$7\frac{1}{2}$-oz can tuna, drained	213 g
$\frac{1}{2}$ cup chopped celery	125 ml
$\frac{3}{4}$ cup shredded Cheddar cheese	175 ml
$\frac{1}{3}$ cup mayonnaise	75 ml
4 to 6 pita pockets	4 to 6

Mash together all ingredients. Fill each pita pocket with mixture. Arrange on baking tray and bake at 350°F (180°C) for 15 minutes.

SALMON PATTIES

7 $\frac{1}{2}$-oz can pink salmon	213 g
3 to 4 medium potatoes	3 to 4
$\frac{1}{2}$ small white onion, chopped	$\frac{1}{2}$
1 egg, chopped	1
pepper to taste	
flour for dusting	
2 tbsp oil for frying	30 ml

Remove bones and skin from salmon. Boil potatoes and mash. Add onion, egg, pepper and salmon to potatoes. Mix together and form into mini-patties. Dust with flour. Fry.
   Serve with ketchup.

SIMPLY DELICIOUS BAKED FISH

2 large eggs, beaten	2
$\frac{1}{2}$ cup milk	125 ml
1 $\frac{1}{2}$ cups bread crumbs	375 ml
$\frac{1}{2}$ tsp garlic powder	2 ml
$\frac{1}{2}$ tsp celery salt	2 ml
2 lbs white fish fillets (sole)	1 kg
pepper to taste	
pinch of cayenne pepper (optional)	

Gently beat eggs and milk. Mix bread crumbs with seasonings. (Add in a few tsp wheat germ if you wish. A pinch of cayenne pepper will add a little zing. Omit if serving to very young children.) Spread seasoned crumbs on clean paper or board. Dip fillets into egg and milk mixture. Roll fillets in bread crumbs.

Fry in pan with butter, oil or cooking spray. Brown on one side. Flip.

Or, bake on oiled cookie sheet in 400°F (200°C) oven for a maximum of 30 minutes. Flip after 15 minutes. Test for readiness after 20 minutes. The thickness of the fillets will alter cooking times. Serve with lemon wedges.

Alternative: Try substituting egg and milk dip with plain yogurt. Dip fillets in yogurt then roll in seasoned bread crumbs.

DIPPY FISH FINGERS

Remember our children's credo, "If you can't dip it, it isn't food."

1 lb white fish	500 g
$\frac{1}{2}$ cup wheat germ	125 ml
$\frac{1}{4}$ cup sesame seeds	50 ml
$\frac{1}{4}$ tsp garlic salt	1 ml
1 large egg	1
2 tbsp milk	30 ml
2 tbsp oil	30 ml
sprinkle of sesame seeds	

Oil baking dish. Chop fish into 1 x 3-inch (2 x 7 cm) fingers. Mix wheat germ, sesame seeds, garlic salt on a plate and set aside. Mix egg with milk and oil in bowl and set aside. Roll individual fish fingers in wheat germ mixture. Dip into egg mixture. Roll in wheat germ mixture one more time. Place on baking sheet and sprinkle with more sesame seeds. Bake at 350°F (180°C) for 12 to 15 minutes.

Serves three to four small children. Serve with lemon wedges and dips.

Dips: Mix 2 tbsp (30 ml) green hamburger relish with 2 tbsp (30 ml) mayonnaise.

Or, mix 1 tsp (5 ml) horseradish with 2 tbsp (30 ml) ketchup.

OVEN BAKED FISH

$\frac{1}{2}$ cup mayonnaise (or $\frac{1}{4}$ cup mayonnaise and $\frac{1}{4}$ cup plain yogurt)	125 ml
$\frac{1}{2}$ tsp marjoram	2 ml
$\frac{1}{2}$ tsp dry mustard	2 ml
pinch cayenne (optional)	
2 tbsp lemon juice	30 ml
2 lbs white fish fillets	1 kg
pepper to taste	
paprika to taste	

Mix all ingredients except fish and paprika. Pour half of mixture in an oiled baking dish. Lay fillets over the mixture. Pour the rest of the mixture over the fish. Sprinkle with paprika. Bake at 500°F (260°C) for 20 minutes.

SPAGHETTI SAUCE FISH

"More sauce please. I can still see the fish."
—Sam (ten years old)

Tomato sauce covers a multitude of good eats. Use it everywhere.

1 lb white fish	500 g
$\frac{1}{2}$ cup corn niblets*	125 ml
$\frac{1}{2}$ cup chopped tomatoes*	125 ml
2 cups spaghetti sauce	500 ml
grated Parmesan cheese	

Pour half the sauce in a baking dish. Spread fish fillets over the sauce. Spread vegetables on top of and around fish. Pour the remaining sauce over the fillets and vegetables. Sprinkle cheese. Bake at 450°F (230°C) for 20 to 25 minutes.

*Note: These two vegetables came out as the vegetables preferred by our little testers for use in this recipe. Do substitute them with your child's favorite vegetables. (Hard vegetables such as broccoli or cauliflower may have to be very lightly steamed in advance.) However, parents be advised, *most* of our testers preferred that no vegetables be used at all or in one child's words, "Why wreck the fish and sauce with vegetables."

CHEESY PATTIES

3 to 4 medium potatoes	3 to 4
1 cup shredded Cheddar cheese	250 ml
1 egg	1
2 green onions, chopped	2
1 tsp chopped parsley	5 ml
$\frac{1}{2}$ cup bread crumbs	125 ml
2 tbsp oil for frying	30 ml

Boil and mash potatoes. Add all ingredients and mix. Shape into bite-size patties. Fry.

Note: Try freezing a few and serve them for breakfast, or pop them into lunchboxes.

CARROT AND APPLE SLAW

4 large carrots, grated	4
1 small red apple, chopped	1
1 tbsp chopped chives	15 ml
$\frac{1}{2}$ tbsp chopped parsley	10 ml
2 tbsp olive oil	30 ml
1 tbsp cider vinegar	15 ml
$\frac{1}{2}$ tsp prepared mustard	2 ml
salt and pepper to taste	

Toss all ingredients together.

Note: Send this salad to school in an airtight container.

DICEY APPLE SLAW

1 red apple, chopped	1
1 green apple, chopped	1
1 tsp lemon juice	5 ml
$\frac{1}{2}$ cup seedless green grapes	125 ml
$\frac{1}{2}$ cup black grapes, seeded	125 ml
$\frac{1}{2}$ bunch watercress, chopped	$\frac{1}{2}$
$\frac{1}{2}$ cup shredded white cabbage	125 ml

$\frac{1}{2}$ cup sour cream	125 ml
salt and pepper to taste	

Sprinkle chopped apples with lemon juice. Halve grapes. Toss all with sour cream and season with salt and pepper.

More or Less

MORE JUICE
- Marinate meat in orange juice, soya sauce, ginger root and garlic.
- Tenderize meat by marinating it in pineapple juice.
- Give turnips and carrots a buzz by cooking in orange juice.
- Cook rice in orange juice.
- In recipes that call for white wine, substitute apple juice.
- Baste roast chicken in a cup of apple juice.
- Use juice plus 1 tbsp (15 ml) of sugar or honey instead of water when preparing jelly. Juices that contain strong enzymes, such as pineapple or mango juice, will prevent the gelatin from setting.
- Make popsicles from juice. (See page 92.)

MORE MILK
- Use milk instead of water when cooking hot cereals.
- Poach chicken and fish in milk.
- Soak liver in milk before cooking. (Discard milk.)
- Defrost fish in milk. (Discard milk.)
- Use milk instead of water when preparing condensed canned soups.
- Make a milk dessert. Combine one cup of fruit-flavored yogurt with gelatin. Chill.
- Add powdered milk to macaroni and cheese dishes.

- Make puddings with milk.
- Coat white fish with plain yogurt and roll in seasoned bread crumbs before cooking.

LESS SALT

- Remove the salt shaker from the table.
- Plug up most of the holes in the salt shaker with grains of uncooked rice.
- Replace table salt with fine herbs—dried basil, parsley, Italian seasoning—experiment!
- Crush sesame seeds and combine with salt in a 50/50 mixture.
- Omit salt from cooking. Replace with dry mustard, herbs, vinegar and lemon juice.
- Buy crackers with unsalted tops. Opt for nuts without salt. Check out the many new products available (e.g., soft drinks) with reduced salt levels.
- Try sodium-reduced soya sauce.
- Use homemade chicken stock instead of heavily salted bouillon cubes or powders.

MORE FRUIT

- Add raisins and berries to salads.
- Add bananas, apple chunks and berries to cereals.
- Add applesauce to cookie and muffin mixes.
- Put chunks of melon or cantaloupe in a blender and serve it as summer soup. (See Summer Lime Fruit Salad, page 96.)
- Add chopped apples, peaches or blueberries to pancake mix.
- Peel and section an orange. Wrap and freeze, and serve as a frosty treat.
- Peel and freeze a banana. (See Banana Dip, page 143.)

- Serve up fruity shakes. (See Smoothies, page 69.)
- Plop berries into ice-cube trays, top-up with juice, freeze and serve in drinks, or as a slippery treat.

MORE VEGETABLES

- To thicken soups, steam vegetables, whirl them in blender and add to any soup.
- Add steamed vegetables to children's favorite pasta. Toss with oil and herbs.
- Keep a bag of frozen mixed vegetables in the freezer. Add a handful to chicken noodle soup. (Start this habit when the children are young.)
- Add chopped celery to chicken and egg salad sandwiches.
- Shred lettuce into sandwiches.
- Serve zucchini, carrot and pumpkin breads as desserts.
- Pour a favorite sauce (spaghetti sauce?) over steamed vegetables and spoon-size pasta.
- Let children add vegetables to different soups.
- Grate a carrot into spaghetti sauce.
- Keep a supply of fresh veggies in the fridge for quick snacks.
- Make an avocado dip and serve with vegetables and or crackers.
- Mash potato with banana. If your child has passed her first birthday, you might want to add a dribble of honey. (Babies under one year should not be given honey.)

MORE FIBER

- Look for fiber in all the right places. A 6-oz (160 g) pear, for example, contains 5 g of fiber.
- Keep a jar full of trail mix in the cupboard. Or make your own mix with sunflower seeds, raisins and two or three types of nuts. Add to salads, curries or serve by the handful.

- Serve cereals as snacks.
- Keep a jar of wheat germ on hand and add it to muffins, cereals, cakes and so on.
- Bulk out hamburgers and meat loaf with bulgur wheat. It swells to 3 to 4 times its size when soaked in boiling water for half an hour.
- Try replacing white flour with whole-wheat flour in many of your frequently used recipes.
- Refried beans make an excellent dip. Add chips or crackers.

GOOD HABITS

- Use canola oil or olive oil whenever possible.
- Replace sour cream with low-fat yogurt.
- Serve ice milk instead of ice cream.
- Switch to mustard instead of mayonnaise on sandwiches.
- Use plain yogurt instead of mayonnaise to "glue" sandwiches together.
- Baked potatoes may replace french fries.

Tofu Treats

It's gooey and it's oozy and it slithers through the fingers just fine. While you're cooking tofu, give your highchair-bound baby a few bits to play with.

Of course the other name for tofu is "soy bean curd." (Unless your child has more than a passing acquaintance with tofu, why enlighten her about tofu's other name?)

Vegetarians swear by the stuff, and who can blame them? It's a good source of protein and calcium (if made with calcium sulfate). It's low in saturated fat and can do just about anything. Tofu has no discernable taste and therefore picks up the taste of other foods nicely. Store it according to the package directions.

Sharon E. McKay

Sneaking "good-for-you" food into your child's diet isn't the best way to introduce new foods, but when push comes to shove, sometimes the best way to introduce a new texture, and a new taste, is just to mix it in with something more palatable. Here are some ways to introduce tofu.

- Bake a potato. Scoop out filling and leave skin intact. Mash the potato with 1 tbsp (15 ml) of tofu and return mixture to the skins. Sprinkle potato with Cheddar cheese. Bake 5 minutes in 300°F (150°C) oven. Cool until it can be handled. Encourage the child to eat the whole potato—skin and all.
- When a recipe calls for sour cream, replace half the recommended amount of cream with mashed tofu.
- To substitute tofu for sour cream, mix 1 cup (250 ml) tofu with 2 tbsp (30 ml) oil and $\frac{1}{4}$ tsp (1 ml) mustard. Blend in food processor until smooth.
- Steam cauliflower. Mash cauliflower with tofu. Top with grated Cheddar cheese. Put under broiler for 1 minute.
- Mash tofu in bowl. Mix with cooked macaroni and cheese. Put in casserole dish. Shred Cheddar cheese on top of macaroni. Top with sliced tomato. Broil.
- See also Tofu Egg Salad (page 79) and Heady Pineapple (page 73).

8

PARTY TIME

In the 1980s children's birthday parties became a rather commercial affair. Here's a typical 80s invitation: "Please drop (fill in name) off at Party Palace at 3:00. Pick him/her up at 5:00."

Home parties often boasted a clown or two, a magician—hey, how about that elephant!

Enter the 90s. It would seem that the ol' cake-and-ice cream birthday parties have returned, complete with games and harassed parents.

••

"I know my party has been really great when my Mom and Dad fall face forward onto the bed and say that next year they both plan to be out of town for my birthday."—An eight-year-old

••

Think about it and then talk about it. What does your child *want* from his or her party?

Most children want to be the FOCUS of the attention. Clowns and dancing bears often divert attention from the birthday child. There may be peer pressure to overcome—"But Mommy, Billy's parents built the deck of the Starship Enterprise in his backyard." (A pox on Billy's parents.) If your family gets dragged into a riveting good game of one-upmanship at this age, you're all in for a rough ride.

Ask your child, "What was the best thing about your last birthday party?" And, "What was the best thing about Jamie's party?"

When asked, most children want a party that shows off their bedroom—"This is where I sleep." And their parents—"This is my father." (Watch a child grow a foot when her pal says, "Your mom is really nice.")

Children do not care, or notice, the condition of the drapes, rugs or furniture. And sometimes they don't even notice what they eat.

••

"I had my six-year-old son's party catered. The sandwiches were all cut into animal shapes and the cheese tray was astonishing. As the children were leaving I asked two little boys which sandwiches they liked best. They looked surprised and said, 'What sandwiches? Didn't we have hot dogs?'"

••

Birthday Tips with Food in Mind
- How irresistible. Send out invitations in a mini-box of cookies.
- If a child says that she has an allergy to a specific food, believe her. No child should be excluded from a party because of a disability. Talk to the child's parents. It might be best if a child with a serious food allergy were to bring her own boxed lunch.
- Instead of place cards use jumbo homemade cookies and write the names of the guests on the cookies with cookie paint.

COOKIE PAINT (ENOUGH FOR 12 TO 15 GIANT COOKIES)

2 egg yolks	2
$\frac{1}{2}$ tsp water	2 ml
variety of food colorings	

Mix yolks with water and divide into egg cups. Add different food coloring to each egg cup. Sugar cookies should be painted before baking. Other cookies may be painted after baking.

••

"Every year my Mom took a picture of me with my birthday cake. I never saw that picture. Now I know why. She put the pictures in a special book, along with notes about who was at my party, what my party dress was like, what Nana and Bubba gave me for a present and so on. On my twenty-first birthday my Mom gave me that book. It's my most treasured possession."

••

Birthday Food

Keep it simple, safe, silly.

Serve the meal (sandwiches, hot dogs, and so on) towards the start of the party. Well-fed children tend to behave a little better. (No promises.) Serve the cake towards the end of the party. Children tend to settle down when they eat. (Not always.)

- Combine several cold cereals with raisins to make a Nuts & Bolts treat. Cap'n Crunch, Shreddies and Corn Pops mixed with pretzels make a good snack. (See page 92.)
- If you serve hot dogs, slit them down the middle to reduce the chance of a child choking. Grapes and peanut butter on white bread, can also pose a problem. However, any

food can choke a running, tumbling and moving child. Make it a rule (but *please* don't make too many rules): "Children must sit up straight when they eat."

GREAT BIRTHDAY FOOD:
Weenies and Beans (page 80)
Pizza Project (page 104)
The Salad Bar (page 105)
Stuff Your Own Potato (page 107)
Meaty Tacos (page 114)

Desserts
"I don't like nuts." "I don't like strawberries." "I don't like ... "

It's true, the picky eater might not even like dessert. Save yourself lots of trouble and let children make their own desserts.

Another advantage of having a make-it-yourself birthday party is that the preparation of the food becomes an activity. This worked so well for us that one year we had a cooking party, using most of these child-simple recipes.

MAKE-IT-YOURSELF CAKE CONES
Save time—don't waste Grandma's homemade-cake recipe on this idea, use a cake mix. I've yet to see a child slowly savor cake cones—they're too yummy. They'll be wolfed down.

Prepare cake batter and pour it into a "cup" or flat-bottomed ice-cream cone. Fill the cone to the halfway mark with batter. DO NOT OVERFILL. Stand the cones up on a cookie sheet or prop them up in a muffin tin. Bake at 350°F (180°C) for 20 to 25 minutes.

Let the children ice and decorate their own cones. Along with the icing, put out bowls of Smarties or M&M's, sprinkles, chocolate chips and so on.

Cake cones are perfect at a backyard birthday party—no napkins, plates or forks. The next time you are at a fast-food restaurant or ice-cream parlor, ask for a cardboard ice-cream holder (a cardboard soft-drink holder will also do). Keep it. Serve the cake cones in the holder.

CHOCOLATE FONDUE

Melt 6 to 8 oz (150 to 250 g) dark chocolate in a double boiler. Pour into a ceramic-bottom fondue pot or dish. Let the children dip and coat their own nuts or fresh fruit (canned fruit is too mushy).

Fruit: Orange or grapefruit sections, peeled and sliced kiwi, cherries with stems intact, strawberries, sliced bananas, seedless grapes, walnuts or Brazil nuts.

Set the chocolate-dipped fruit on waxed paper to dry.

For safety's sake, supervise the dipping—one little dipper at a time. Depending on the age of the children, you may not want to have the candle under the fondue pot lit.

The quantity mentioned will serve four children adequately.

BANANA DIP

Wrap peeled bananas in foil and freeze for 1 hour. (One per party guest.)

Put a popsicle stick in one end of the frozen banana.

Give each child a banana to dip in melted chocolate.

Lay out yummy toppers such as granola, sprinkles, chopped nuts, chopped cherries, on separate plates. Lay the chocolate-coated bananas on waxed paper and pop them back into the freezer to set. They'll be ready to eat after two games of pin-the-tail-on-the-donkey and one game of musical chairs.

YOGURT DIP

Arrange fresh fruit on a tray beside a bowl of fruit-flavored yogurt, and put brown sugar on a small plate. Let the children dip the fruit in the yogurt and then roll it in the brown sugar.

BANANA SPLIT

Give each child a peeled and split banana in a bowl, plus three small scoops of ice cream each, and let them do the work.

In separate bowls lay out: chopped nuts, shredded coconut, sprinkles, cherries, chopped strawberries, orange sections, chocolate chips and so on. If sauces are commercially bought, choose those that come in small squeeze-bottles, or transfer them to plastic ketchup or honey bottles.

Don't forget to put out a big bowl of fluffy whipped cream.

JULIE'S CHOCOLATE SAUCE

1 tbsp cocoa	15 ml
2 tbsp butter	30 ml
$\frac{1}{3}$ cup hot water	75 ml
1 cup sugar	250 ml
2 tbsp corn syrup	30 ml
$\frac{1}{8}$ tsp salt	.5 ml
$\frac{1}{2}$ tsp vanilla	2 ml

Combine all ingredients, except vanilla, in medium pot. Cook until boiling, stirring constantly. Reduce heat and simmer for 3 minutes. Remove from heat and stir in vanilla. Cool and serve.

Note: Sauce is tasty over pears as well as ice cream.

FROSTY FRUIT CANDIES

Frosted fruits might be used to decorate the birthday cake, circle the base of a candlestick for a very sophisticated party (e.g., she's turning ten) or eaten as is.

Whisk two egg whites until frothy. Lay out fruits on a cookie sheet or cooling rack. (Strawberries, sliced or whole, firm berries of all kinds, and peeled and sliced kiwi fruits work well.) Coat the fruits with the egg whites using a small artists' brush. Dip or sprinkle confectioners' sugar over the fruits. Let sit.

To separate the egg yolk from the white, crack the egg and drop it into a child's clean hand. Ask the child to open his fingers slowly and let the white of the egg drip into a bowl. (Disgusting? No. Kids love it.)

STRAWBERRY SANDWICH

Take one box of graham crackers, a square carton of strawberry frozen yogurt and another small carton of vanilla ice cream. Open the cartons and slice the ice cream into small cracker size squares. Arrange on a plate.

Take one cracker and cover it with one square of frozen vanilla ice cream, followed by one square of strawberry yogurt. Ram another cracker on top. Eat.

MELON BOAT

This is a make-ahead project that small children can help with.

Cut a honeydew melon—or if you are expecting many guests, a small watermelon—in half. Take a sharp knife and make zigzags around the edges. Scoop out the melon meat with a melon scooper, making little balls. Fill the boat with cherries, strawberries, sliced pears and plums, grapes and melon balls. Sprinkle with melon juice. Use as a centerpiece. Give each of the children a spoon and let them dig in.

Drinks

••
Tip: To get more juice out of oranges or grapefruit, stick fruit in the microwave on high (100%) for 20 seconds before squeezing.
••

SNOW CONES #1

Put 3 tbsp (45 ml) of undiluted raspberry or strawberry concentrated juice in the blender with four ice cubes. Whirl. Decorate with a fresh strawberry and a mint leaf.

SNOW CONES #2

Fill small paper cups with crushed ice. Offer the children two toppings of any undiluted (concentrated) juice. Raspberry concentrate is a favorite.

JUICE POP

Pour 3 tbsp (45 ml) of juice concentrate (any flavor) into a glass. Gently add club soda. Decorate with an orange section and a maraschino cherry.

RASPBERRY WHIRL

Put one individual serving of plain yogurt in a blender. Add 3 tbsp (45 ml) (more or less to taste) of undiluted raspberry concentrate. Whirl.

GRAPEFRUIT SURPRISE

Slice the top off a grapefruit. Scoop out the pulp. Blend part of the pulp with undiluted orange concentrate and a scoop of vanilla ice cream. Pour back into the grapefruit shell. Seconds before serving, top it up with club soda for that certain "volcano" effect.

PEACHES & CREAM TREAT

1 cup milk	250 ml
1 cup sliced peaches	250 ml
1 pint vanilla ice cream	500 ml
3 tbsp lemonade concentrate	45 ml

Whirl all in blender.

PUNCH-UP ORANGE

2 cups grapefruit juice	500 ml
juice of 1 orange	1
juice of 1 lemon	1
$\frac{1}{2}$ cup sugar	125 ml
2 cups club soda (or water)	500 ml

Mix grapefruit juice with juice of orange and lemon. Add sugar. Slowly pour in club soda or water. Garnish with chunks of orange and grapefruit.

PUNCHY PUNCH

2 cups grapefruit juice	500 ml
2 cups pineapple juice	500 ml
juice of 2 oranges	2
juice of 1 lemon	1

$\frac{1}{2}$ cup sugar	125 ml
2 to 3 cups club soda	500 to 750 ml

Mix grapefruit juice with pineapple juice. Add orange and lemon juice and sugar. Slowly mix in club soda. Garnish with cherries.

Theme Parties

TEDDY BEAR TEA PARTY, DOLLIES WELCOME
(Ages 2 to 4)
Use ginger-boy cookie cutters to make teddy-bear-shaped sandwiches.

Make jello in a shallow pan and use cookie cutters to make teddy-bear-shaped jello treats.

Serve apple juice or warm apple cider from a teapot.

DINOSAUR PARTY
(Ages 3 to 5)
Serve brontosaurus burgers (giant hamburgers).

Give out miniature, plastic dinosaurs, point to a sand or dirt pile in the backyard and suggest the children excavate for bones. (Tuck a few clean chicken bones in the earth.)

Since excavating is a dirty business, sprinkle hot chocolate powder over chocolate cup cakes and call it "dirt."

INDIANA JONES PARTY
(Ages 5 to 7)
Set up a tent in the basement. Dim the lights. Use foil and a flashlight for the campfire. Dig out the Hallowe'en decorations. Instead of wasting a small fortune on the take-home goodie bag, hand out disposable two-dollar flashlights and let the kids take them home. Indiana is always after a treasure.

Put gold-foil-covered chocolates in a treasure box. Mix them in with that old junk jewelry that you've been meaning to get rid of.

Put tiny, plastic spiders in an ice-cube tray. Add water. Freeze. Pop into the pop.

Remember, Indiana doesn't like snakes, so be sure to have plenty of (fake) snakes around.

Scary Party (Hallowe'en)
(Ages 5 to 8)
No need to go out trick-or-treating. Bring the fun indoors.

Put stuffed olives in an ice-cube tray, add water, freeze. Add the "eyeballs" to drinks. Best served in a clear drink.

Eyeball Jelly

1 small tin lichee nuts (found in oriental grocery stores)
8 raisins

Drain 8 lichee nuts (eyeballs) and insert raisin (pupils) in nuts.

1 package lime jelly powder (4-serving size)	
$\frac{3}{4}$ cup boiling water	175 ml
$\frac{1}{2}$ cup cold water	125 ml
ice cubes	

Dissolve jelly in boiling water. Combine cold water and ice cubes to a total of $1\frac{1}{4}$ cups (300 ml). Add to jelly. Stir until it thickens. Remove any unmelted ice. Refrigerate for 15 minutes or so. Pour into 4 small, clear glasses to the halfway mark. Pop one eyeball into each glass. Pour more jelly into the glass and insert a second eyeball close to the top of the glass. Chill at least 1 hour.

GROSS-OUTS
Bat's eyes—peeled black grapes
Maggots on a log—cream cheese in celery sticks dotted with raisins
Bat wings dipped in blood—blue corn chips with dip (add two drops of red food coloring to favorite dip)

SCARY GAMES
Blindfold a child. (Little ones can simply close their eyes.) Have one child (at a time) dip his hands into: cold spaghetti mixed with a tablespoon of oil; raw liver; cold beans. Ask the children to describe what their hands are in. Put treasures wrapped in foil in the ghoulish food.

Safety Tips
- No toothpicks. Ever. They stick in throats and have no place at any party. Use straight pretzels if you need to poke anything. At the very least, use long, plastic swizzle sticks. Avoid straws, too.
- Remove dead balloons promptly. Children often stretch a broken bit of balloon over their mouths to make a popping sound. That small bit of balloon can be sucked into the throat and conform to the shape of the throat. Very scary. Another point about balloons—a baby's hearing can be damaged if a balloon is popped very close to his or her ear.
- Long hair and birthday candles do not mix. Tie back the birthday child's hair.
- Since you cannot watch all the guests all the time, be sure your home is adequately childproofed. If grand-moms or other moms are coming, tuck their purses up on a high shelf. As any toddler knows, there are good-ies in Grandma's purse. (There may also be heart pills.)
- Stock up on Bandaids.
- Ask in advance about the party guests' allergies.

9

TRAVELING WITH THE PICKY EATER

Children become ravenous the moment they fasten their seat belts—or so it would seem. A parent could keep a can of chocolate-covered caterpillars in the glove compartment and the kids would beg for it. For some reason, a child who normally won't eat something as reasonable as eggs, will eat shoe leather in the car.

Traveling with a picky eater really tests the whole notion of parenthood. Away from home a parent has to contend not only with a child who eats only smooth peanut butter on brown (if it's raining and there was a full moon last night), but also with an outside world which lives only to give advice.

"If my daughter doesn't eat everything on her plate, I smack her." (Waitress at a roadside diner)

"You give in to that child too much. Just serve his dinner and if he doesn't eat—let him starve." (Great Aunt Maude, who does not have children)

"If he doesn't behave at the table, make him eat with the dog." (Your teenage brother)

"I never used to let *you* get away with this kind of behavior." (Grandpa)

"If she won't eat, just spank her. That's the trouble with kids today, they don't get spanked enough." (Lady in the next booth)

"Look lady, the cook only makes sandwiches with butter. If your kid doesn't want butter on his sandwich, he can scrape it off." (Waiter)

"We don't divide meals here." (Waiter)

"The sauce comes with the hamburger. It's how hamburgers were intended to be served." (Waiter)

"I'm sorry, but we're out of the children's meal on this flight. Do you suppose she'll enjoy a few mussels followed by grilled swordfish with lemon-rice pilaf?" (Helpful flight attendant)

Parents are the first, and often the only, line of defense a child has. Well-intentioned grandparents, aunties and/or hosts sometimes take a very aggressive stance when confronted by a child who will not eat the food they serve. Many take the refusal of food very personally. Head this off at the pass if you can.

• •

"My mother takes great pride in her cooking, especially her spaghetti. So when my six-year-old wouldn't touch it, my mother was upset. I wanted the two to have a good relationship and that wouldn't happen if they became locked in a power struggle over food. So I found that the best way to get through the holiday was to cook a little dinner for my son a half-hour earlier than our dinner."

• •

If you're convinced that your child's nutrition will be totally messed up, talk to your child's doctor or the pharmacist about a kid-type vitamin pill. Normally vitamin pills are not recommended for children who are eating a balanced diet, and pills given over a short period seldom have much effect. But if the pill will make you, the parent, more relaxed, then go for it.

There are a few points to remember when traveling with all children—picky eaters especially.

Traveling by Car

Sticking two children and assorted pets, both real and stuffed, into a six-by-three-foot space is nothing short of madness. Don't expect to survive the ordeal without a few battle scars.

Five minutes after you've pulled out of a rest station, expect to hear, "I hafta go pee." "I forgot Teddy in the store." "Mommy, was Billy allowed to take the ketchup from the restaurant?"

Pack your sense of humor. And realize that your child will not eat "balanced" meals during a holiday.

Tips

- Bring a cooler filled with juice. (DO NOT leave the cooler out, open and unattended. Little children have been known to crawl in and suffocate.)
- Fill a plastic jug halfway with the favored non-carbonated drink. Freeze it. Top up the jug the next day. The bottom half will act like a giant ice cube and keep the drink cool all day.
- Give each child his own water jug. Make sure it's spill proof and keep the water level down to the halfway mark—just in case.
- Pack your child's lunchbox with non-salty treats that he or she may dip into at will and without your permission. Dried fruits, crackers and cereal are all treats that appease a hunger but don't fill up a tummy.
- Give your child a snack just before entering a restaurant—perhaps fruit. Service is never fast enough for small children and fruit is better to snack on than a basket of white rolls.

Quick stops into fast-food restaurants along the highway are a given. Fast-food meals do provide some nutritional value but normally are woefully short on vegetables. No matter. A meal without vegetables here and there will do no harm. If the plan is to be on the road for weeks, however, then you may have a problem. Not only will your child not be eating an adequate diet, but he or she will be adding on a lot of empty calories (and in the backseat of a car there's little opportunity to work them off). The result will be hyperactivity (if the child is consuming drinks containing caffeine), lethargy and general misbehavior. It's really important to stop in at food markets along the way and replenish the picnic basket and cooler with fresh fruits, vegetables, yogurt and nutritious snacks.

Traveling by Air
Choose your seat with care. Bulkhead seats provide space for a cot carrier (provided by the airline). However, food trays are fixed to the seat, making it difficult to attend to children.

Bring your own baby food. Some airlines do provide food, some don't. Either way, the food they provide may not be what you want for your baby.

Ask about the menu during check-in. There are many food options available for children.

Foreign Parts
On the road, in a plane, on a train—children are often uneasy. Even the most secure child will miss the security and familiarity of her own environment. The operative words here are "security" and "familiarity." Children can be taken anywhere if they know that their mom or dad will keep them safe. As for the "familiarity" part—well, you may have to bring that with you.

Bring your own food with you! OK, you can't schlep a lot of food around the world. Besides, there are pesky laws and such that make the transfer of food across borders a tad difficult—as it should be. However, you *can* bring foods like freeze-dried chicken noodle soup and powdered chocolate.

• •

"We traveled through China with our five-year-old. There were days when he ate very little. We were both comforted by a cup of Lipton's Chicken Noodle Soup* at the end of the day. The soup reminded us of home and somehow prepared us for a new day of adventures."

*Any brand of freeze-dried soup will do. However, don't bring canned soups with you. Security in some airports will not allow tins on a flight.

• •

Study the information given to you at the point of entry. Better yet, stop in at a library or, if possible, the embassy before leaving and read up on local diseases, customs and laws. Should you eat the salads? Drink the water? When in doubt—don't. (Watch out for ice cubes. They may not be made of purified water.)

Once upon a time, before children, it was possible to try out the local food from street vendors in far-away cities. If you have children traveling with you, then your responsibilities include their safety. A parent simply can't afford to get sick when in a foreign city with small children in tow.

• •

"My husband and I do not eat the same food when we are traveling with our children, nor do we taste off each other's plates. Our children are small. We would all be in deep trouble if both my husband and I were to develop food poisoning at the same time."

• •

Tips

- In some countries street vendors will rebottle drinks using unsafe water and press on a new cap. When in doubt, it's best to buy canned pop for your children. (Your children will think they are in heaven.)
- If food is meant to be hot, eat it hot, not lukewarm. If food is meant to be cold, eat it cold.
- Depending on the country you're in, buy some of your food from the local food store. In First World countries, and many Second World countries, the local food stores have "safe" food. In Developing World countries you may want to go prepared. Contact the Canadian embassy and ask for advice. (This may sound a tad over-cautious—after all, we travel to learn. However, children get sick fast. A sick child at home is awful. A sick child away from home in a country that does not have familiar medical treatments, or in which your native language is not spoken, is hell.)
- Many countries do not refrigerate their meat as we do. Unless you know otherwise, avoid buying meat in small shops. Enjoy it instead in well-chosen restaurants, or become temporary vegetarians.

Ten Things Not to Say to Your Picky Eater

1 "If you don't eat you'll go to bed."

2 "If you eat all your vegetables you can have dessert."

3 "You're not getting up from the table until you have eaten your dinner."

4 "Clean that plate."

5 "You're lucky that you have a meal. Some children don't have anything to eat. Now EAT."

6 "Just eat the vegetables."

7 "Come on. Open up. That's my girl. Pleeeeeease. Just one bite."

8 "I've had enough of this. It took me two hours to make this. Just eat it."

9 "You liked it yesterday. What's your problem?"

10 "You're such a good boy. You ate everything. Mommy loves you."

Index

A
After-School Apple, 90
allergies, 21, 61
APPLES,
  After-School Apple, 90
  Apple Juice Pork, 113
  Baby Waldorf, 106-7
  Carrot and Apple Slaw, 133
  Dicey Apple Slaw, 133-34
Apricot Smoothie, 72
asparagus, 115-16
avocados, 23

B
BABY FOOD,
  commercial, 20-21
  for toddlers, 31
Baby Waldorf, 106-7
bacon, 22, 81, 99
Bag Salad, 97
bagels, 77-78
Baked Potato to Go, 80
BANANAS, 28
  Banana Dip, 143
  Banana Pancakes, 66
  Banana Smoothie, 70
  Banana Split, 144
  Banana Split Brekky, 65
  Banana and Strawberry
    Whip, 70
  Best Banana, 70-71
  Better Butter Banana, 72
  Choco-Banana, 71
  kabobs, 63

  and peanut butter, 82
  smoothies, 69-72
  Terrific Tyler, 70
  Yogurt Pops #2, 93
BEANS, 64
  Refried Bean Dip, 89, 137
  Weenies and Beans, 80-81
BEEF,
  Beef Kabobs, 103-4
  Dot's Spaghetti Sauce, 118-19
  Meaty Tacos, 114-15
  Treasure Meat Balls, 116-17
beets, 122
Best Banana, 70-71
Better Butter Banana, 72
Blue Cheese Dip, 103
Blueberry Pancakes, 66
breakfast bars, 56, 67-68
Brekky Bars, 67
BROCCOLI,
  Broccoli and Cheese
    Sauce, 101
  Broccoli Trees, 99
  Green Potatoes, 123
  Green Soup, 123
  Trees in the Forest, 115-16
Bruschetta, 76
bulgur wheat, 137

C
CABBAGE,
  Dicey Apple Slaw, 133-34
  Yo-Slaw, 100
cakes, 142-43
Camembert Cheese Dip, 87
CARROTS, 27, 28, 31
  Carrot and Apple Slaw, 133
  Carrot and Pineapple Salad, 97

159

Carrot and Apple Slaw, 133
Carrot and Pineapple Salad, 97
Dicey Apple Slaw, 133-34
Jungle Salad, 95-96
Mini Salad Bar, 105-6
Orange Head Salad, 98-99
salad bars, 57, 59, 105-6
Salad in a Pocket, 106
Salad with Quick Fruit
  Dressing, 96-97
Summer Lime Fruit Salad, 96
tahini dressing, 106
wrapped in lettuce, 82
Yo-Slaw, 100
SALMON,
  Elegant Salmon, 81
  Salmon Patties, 129
SALT,
  in baby food, 21, 22, 23
  reducing use of, 135
Sam's Chicken Cutlets, 120-21
SANDWICHES, 82-84
  Cream Cheese and
    Pineapple Dots, 80
  Curry in a Bagel, 77-78
  Elegant Salmon, 81
  Flat Fried Cheese, 79
  I-Love-You Cream Cheese, 81
  See also PITA FILLINGS
SAUCES,
  Broccoli and Cheese
    Sauce, 101
  Dot's Spaghetti Sauce, 118-19
  Julie's Chocolate Sauce, 144
  Spaghetti Sauce Fish, 131-32
  Zippy Tomato Sauce, 120
sausages, 22
seeds. *See* NUTS AND SEEDS

shellfish, 57, 61
Simply Delicious Baked
  Fish, 129-30
smoothies, 69-74
Snappy Cheese Sticks, 86-87
Snow Cones, 146
SOUPS, 52, 134, 136, 155
  Cool Red and Green
    Summer Soup, 124-25
  Green Soup, 123
  Mom's Chicken Soup, 124
  Pink Soup, 122
sour cream, 88, 137
soy, 61
SPAGHETTI, 63
  Spaghetti Pie, 119-20
Spaghetti Sauce Fish, 131-32
Spinach Squares, 110
Square Popcorn, 85
stir-fries, 102
STRAWBERRIES, 31
  Banana and Strawberry
    Whip, 70
  Frozen Berry, 71
  Fruity Pops, 92
  Strawberry Sandwich, 145
  Strawberry Smoothie, 71
  Terrific Tyler, 70
Stuff Your Own Potato, 107
SUGAR, 16
  in baby food, 21, 22, 23
Summer Lime Fruit
  Salad, 96

T

TACO FILLINGS,
  Food for Toads, 113-14
  Meaty Tacos, 114-15